The Information-Powered School

Public Education Network

American Association
of School Librarians

EDITED BY
Sandra Hughes-Hassell
AND
Anne Wheelock

AMERICAN LIBRARY ASSOCIATION
Chicago and London
2001

While extensive effort has gone into ensuring the reliability of information appearing in this book, the publisher makes no warranty, express or implied, on the accuracy or reliability of the information, and does not assume and hereby disclaims any liability to any person for any loss or damage caused by errors or omissions in this publication.

Cover photo by Leslie Slavin.
Courtesy of National Library Power Program

Text design by Dianne Rooney

Composition by the dotted i using Sabon and Myriad typefaces in QuarkXPress 4.04 for the Macintosh

Printed on 50-pound white offset, a pH-neutral stock, and bound in 10-point cover stock by Data Reproductions

The paper used in this publication meets the minimum requirements of American National Standard for Information Sciences—Permanence of Paper for Printed Library Materials, ANSI Z39.48-1992. ∞

Library of Congress Cataloging-in-Publication Data

The information-powered school / Public Education Network and American
   Association of School Librarians ; edited by Sandra Hughes-Hassell, Anne
   Wheelock.
      p.   cm.
   Includes index.
   ISBN 0-8389-3514-1
      1. Library Power (Program)   2. School libraries—Standards—United States.
   3. Instructional materials centers—Standards—United States.   4. Media programs
   (Education)—Standards—United States.   5. Information literacy—Standards—
   United States.   6. Curriculum planning—United States.   I. Hughes-Hassell,
   Sandra.   II. Wheelock, Anne.   III. Public Education Network.   IV. American
   Association of School Librarians.
   Z675.S3 I4265 2001
   027.8′0973—dc21   2001022561

Printed in the United States of America.

05   04   03   5   4   3   2

Dedicated to the memory of

Marian D. Usalis (1944–1999)

Former Library Power Director
Cleveland Education Fund

CONTENTS

PREFACE

As every teen with a pager or a Discman can tell you, we live in a society rich with information, which technology has made available instantaneously at the touch of a button. To succeed—indeed, merely to function—in such a world, students must learn the complex set of skills that comprise information literacy.

Helping students become information literate has been at the heart of school library media services since the publication of *Information Power* in 1988. Library Power, a ten-year initiative of the DeWitt Wallace–Reader's Digest Fund, put those ideas to the test under the toughest of circumstances, in 700 schools serving more than 1 million students in impoverished communities around the country.

Library Power developed a new, more challenging vision for school librarianship by ensuring that all learners in the school—adults as well as children—have the resources and supports they need to become effective users of information and ideas. School library media specialists increased their effectiveness and credibility as collaborators and teachers, not just as keepers of books. In essence, Library Power empowered school library media specialists to lead their schools in a change process. Evaluation data from the program indicates increases in leadership, political awareness, advocacy, and interpersonal skills.

THE INFORMATION-POWERED SCHOOL draws on tools and experiences of the Library Power project to help you bring to life the mission of Information Power in your school. Gathering the expertise of project participants, editors Sandra Hughes-Hassell, assistant professor at Drexel University and the director of Philadelphia's Library Power project, and Anne Wheelock, case study writer for the University of Wisconsin's National Program Evaluation of Library Power, have created a hands-on guide with some forty templates, checklists, and forms to support the implementation of *Information Power*.

The subtitle of the 1998 revision of *Information Power* is, "Building Partnerships for Learning." Library Power itself was a national partnership between the Public Education Network (PEN) and AASL. On the local level, Library Power connected local education funds (LEFs) and 35 partner school districts in nineteen communities across the country.

The *Information Power: Building Partnerships for Learning* creators—a joint committee of AASL and Association for Educational Communications and Technology—envisioned an ultimate goal of helping all students become full members of the learning community. PEN shares this goal by working to educate the nation about the relationship between school quality and the quality of community and public life.

The success of Library Power underscores our belief that communities can—and *will*—rise to meet the significant reform challenges of some of the nation's poorest schools. The change was information-powered, and the school library media center was at the heart of it. Our dream is that the tools and advice of THE INFORMATION-POWERED SCHOOL will help you energize your learning community and transform your school to ensure that all learners are prepared for success in the Information Age of the twenty-first century.

WENDY D. PURIEFOY
President,
Public Education Network

JULIE A. WALKER
Executive Director,
American Association of School Librarians

1 Using the *Information-Powered School*

Anne Wheelock

Across the country, educators, community leaders, and parents are asking: How can we best use our resources so that all students will achieve in school? What can we do so that our students learn the skills they need to succeed as citizens and workers in the twenty-first century? What kinds of schools help all children develop as lifelong lovers of learning?

Our response: Information-Powered schools!

Information Power: Building Partnerships for Learning is a powerful tool schools "can use to foster the active, authentic learning that today's researchers and practitioners recognize as vital to helping students become independent, information-literate, lifelong learners" (AECT and AASL, 1998, p. ix). Grounded in a vision of students and teachers as active and engaged information users, *Information Power: Building Partnerships for Learning* puts school library media programs at the center of learning and catalyzes changes in teaching and learning that support improved student work.

Information Power: Building Partnerships for Learning draws schools into resource-rich teaching and learning. Working together, teachers and school library media specialists establish collegial relationships that support collaborative planning and teaching. They use curriculum mapping and collection mapping to connect classroom goals and school library media resources. They engage in ongoing professional development and professional reflec-

tion. And, they partner with community members to refurbish school library facilities and integrate technology into the curriculum. In sum, *Information Power: Building Partnerships for Learning* energizes teaching, learning, and collaboration within the school and the broader community.

What does this mean to the daily life of students and teachers? As new routines, practices, and ways of thinking about student learning replace the old, visitors see:

Students engaged in extended inquiry-based individual and group projects that incorporate information literacy skills.

Students using library media resources and services both during and beyond the school day for multiple purposes, including research, enrichment, and personal enjoyment.

School library media specialists and teachers sharing responsibility for planning, teaching, and assessing student learning.

Teachers and school library media specialists meeting on a regular basis to design and write curriculum, plan instructional units, and make decisions about the library collection.

School library media specialists and teachers "mapping" the curriculum to avoid overlap of topics, foster greater curriculum coherence, and identify resources that enable students to use their own learning styles and abilities to solve complex information problems.

Teachers and school library media specialists expanding their professional knowledge and skills as a team, especially in the areas of inquiry, technology, and assessment.

Evidence of community-wide involvement in and support for the school library media program.

Who Can Benefit from This Tool Kit?

If *Information Power: Building Partnerships for Learning's* vision of teaching and learning appeals to you, and if you're wondering what you can do to realize this vision, *The Information-Powered School* is for you. Implementing new practice depends on developing new ways of looking at schools, learning new skills, and understanding new knowledge. This tool kit provides examples of how real schools and communities have used *Information Power: Building Partnerships for Learning* to advance improvements in teaching and learning for all students.

Getting Oriented: Lessons Learned from the National Library Power Program

Grounding this tool kit is a set of research-based "lessons learned" from the National Library Power Program. Library Power, a ten-year, $40-million initiative of the DeWitt Wallace–Reader's Digest Fund, now the Wallace–Reader's Digest Funds, concentrated on improving teaching and learning through revitalizing elementary and middle school library media programs in nineteen communities across the country. These nineteen communities had several things in common: they had developed a vision for improving teaching and learning through the library media program; they were mobilizing board community support for their vision; and they had made a commitment to full-time school library media specialists. Library Power eventually operated in approximately 700 schools and affected more than 400,000 students.

The Library Power program was built on the recommendations of *Information Power* (ALA, 1988) and evolved to reflect the principles and practices described in *Information Power: Building Partnerships for Learning*. Evaluation reports and the opinions of project directors, school library leadership, and staff from the American Association of School Librarians and the Public Education Network involved with Library Power attest to its success, and suggest that practitioners implementing *Information Power: Building Partnerships for Learning* can benefit from the lessons learned from the Library Power experience. In particular:

Successful implementation of *Information Power: Building Partnerships for Learning* will depend on high-level commitment and leadership. Commitment from key decision makers in the school, including the principal, school library media specialist, and teacher leaders, will be critical to initiating, nurturing, and sustaining such a complex vision as the one articulated in *Information Power: Building Partnerships for Learning*.

Professional development and collaboration count. Professional development and collaboration will be the key means of establishing a professional culture that fosters improved teaching and resource-rich student learning.

Information Power: Building Partnerships for Learning complements school reform initiatives that involve students in inquiry. The principles of *Information Power: Building Partnerships for Learning* will help teachers and administrators address concerns they have about standards, student achievement, and accountability.

The Information-Powered school benefits from partnerships between schools and the community. Community change agents will play a vital role in mobilizing broad support for school library media programs and raising private support to supplement public funding.

Implementing *Information Power: Building Partnerships for Learning* requires a long-term commitment. Stable leadership over time will help ensure success. Planning and strategizing will set the stage for implementing a comprehensive program. Visible changes in facilities and collections will stimulate deeper changes that result in better teaching and learning.

Getting Started: What Does This Tool Kit Have to Offer?

Moving *Information Power: Building Partnerships for Learning* from an abstract vision to real life practice is a long-term commitment. It requires not just hard work, but focused work. To help you introduce new ideas to others, identify needs, plan for and test out new practices, allocate resources in new ways, and refine your work, this tool kit offers you a variety of tools, including:

Library Power Lessons—suggestions for planning and implementing *Information Power: Building Partnerships for Learning* principles and practices, based on what Library Power schools and communities learned.

Library Power Tools—checklists, surveys, and planning forms to help assess the status of current practice and plan for new practice.

Featured resources, including Web resources, to help you learn more about particular aspects of *Information Power: Building Partnerships for Learning*. Use these resources to deepen your own knowledge about *Information Power: Building Partnerships for Learning* principles and to prepare your school for new practice. Ask your colleagues to use these resources to stimulate professional conversations and decision making about implementing *Information Power: Building Partnerships for Learning* in your school.

Just as no one *Information Power: Building Partnerships for Learning* principle stands alone, no one practice or tool in this tool kit stands alone. Each practice reinforces all the others. This means you will find that some material from one chapter relates to material in other chapters. Tools for mapping the school curriculum, for example, support collection development and collaborative planning. Practices in community engagement mesh with approaches to refurbishing facilities. Strategies for resourcing your library media program complement suggestions for professional development.

Constructing Your Own Information-Powered School Library Media Program

This tool kit begins with suggestions for mobilizing leadership and human resources to begin building your own Information-Powered school library media program. It ends with ideas for developing additional resources for sustaining school and school library media program reforms. However, in practice, one program component does not follow another in neat linear sequence. Rather, building an Information-Powered school library media program involves introducing all aspects of the program simultaneously. The ways in which particular program components take hold will vary from school to school. To use this tool kit most effectively and develop a broad understanding of *Information Power: Building Partnerships for Learning* as a whole, we suggest reading the entire tool kit from beginning to end before launching your own Information-Powered program. Then we hope you will return to it at frequent intervals to use the tools and ideas it contains.

This tool kit is meant to be used! We hope you will adopt or adapt the tools it contains to suit your own school, district, and community. Good luck!

Featured Resources for Further Information

American Association of School Librarians and Association for Educational Communications and Technology. 1998. *Information Power: Building Partnerships for Learning*. Chicago: ALA.

American Association of School Librarians and Association for Educational Communications and Technology. 1999. *A Planning Guide for Information Power: Building Partnerships for Learning*. Chicago: AASL.

Web Resources

American Association of School Librarians. 2000. *Learning through the Library.*
    http://www.ala.org/aasl/learning/

American Association of School Librarians. 2000. Resource Guides for School Library Media Programs.
    http://www.ala.org/aasl/resources/

DeWitt Wallace–Reader's Digest Funds. *Library Power: Strategies for Enriching Teaching and Learning in America's Public Schools.*
    http://www.wallacefunds.org/publications/pub_library/index.htm

Public Education Network. 2000. *Library Power Resources.*
    http://www.PublicEducation.org/resources/library.htm

2 Leadership and the Practitioner

Sandra Hughes-Hassell and Anne Wheelock,
with the Paterson Education Fund

The successful implementation of *Information Power: Building Partnerships for Learning* is as much about "people power" as about new school structures or even new materials or facilities. Leadership for the Information-Powered school is collaborative, creating a wave of energy and purpose that provides everyone with a clear vision of what a school library media program based on *Information Power: Building Partnerships for Learning* will look like and how it will benefit students. It generates excitement and inspires others to become engaged in the work of creating a dynamic, effective, student-centered school library media program.

Collaborative leadership:

Draws on the knowledge, skills, and experiences of many people to accomplish multiple, complex tasks.

Engages supporters from diverse constituencies in the school and larger community.

Involves professionals with diverse perspectives and areas of expertise in sharing responsibilities.

Focuses on creating a shared vision for the school library media program.

Allows for reflection and continuous feedback on the implementation process and strategies.

Guiding Principle: Leadership for implementing *Information Power: Building Partnerships for Learning* rests with a variety of participants, including the school library media spe-

cialist, the school's technology coordinator, the principal, teachers, students, and community members. Whatever their role, all participants share a commitment to a vision of teaching and learning grounded in information literacy and view learning as a process that engages students and teachers alike in using a rich array of information resources to solve authentic, complex problems.

The School Library Media Specialist as Information Power Leader

At the school level, no one makes more difference to the implementation of *Information Power: Building Partnerships for Learning* than the school library media specialist. The success of *Information Power: Building Partnerships for Learning* depends on the school library media specialist's ability to assume a visible, proactive leadership role.

To successfully implement *Information Power: Building Partnerships for Learning,* school library media specialists must go well beyond the traditional role of "keepers of the books." They must serve as teachers, staff developers, curriculum planners, and instructional leaders. They must bring their special expertise in information literacy and resource-based instruction to the leadership team, to professional relationships with individual teachers and groups of teachers, and to classroom practice that is extended to the library media center. Whether showing connections between information-based learning and the skills students will need in the twenty-first century, or promoting the staff's use of technology, school library media specialists must demonstrate commitment and dedication to the vision articulated in *Information Power: Building Partnerships for Learning*.

Leadership for school library media specialists involves "leading from the middle." This type of leadership is about influencing people to work willingly for group goals. Leading from the middle includes coaching others to do for themselves, acting as a sounding board for key decision makers, bringing people together, and taking the risk of leading (Herrin, 1993).

As the *Information Power* leader, school library media specialists must:

Provide leadership through professional knowledge and expertise, often as facilitator of the school's Information Power team.

Initiate and sustain communication with teachers, administrators, and parents about all aspects of *Information Power: Building Partnerships for Learning*, including the value of the *Information Literacy Standards for Student Learning* to lifelong learning.

Reach out to teachers, administrators, staff, students, and parents to involve as many people as possible in the implementation of both *Information Power: Building Partnerships for Learning* and the *Information Literacy Standards for Student Learning*.

Schedule collaborative planning time with teachers and facilitate the development of collaborative units, teaching plans, and assessments.

Teach students and teachers *information literacy skills* and show how these skills are integral to subject matter learning in all areas.

Work on subject area and grade-level teams and committees at the building, district, and state level to develop curriculum and establish learning goals and objectives that incorporate information literacy skills.

Work with the Information Power team to reflect on data describing the school library media program.

Before embarking on the implementation of *Information Power: Building Partnerships for Learning*, school library media specialists need to:

Understand the vision described in *Information Power: Building Partnerships for Learning*. Know its purpose and be able to explain how it will benefit students, teachers, and community members. Know the research link between school library media programs and student achievement.

Know the current library media program. Identify strengths and weaknesses.

Gain the support of the principal through advocacy. Show how a school library media program based on *Information Power: Building Partnerships for Learning* will help the principal achieve his or her schoolwide goals.

Identify teachers who are opinion leaders in the school and engage them in the decision-making process. Include these teachers on the Information Power team.

Be aware of other instructional and administrative changes taking place in the school. Many of the current school reform efforts focus on standards, student achievement, and accountability. Identify how *Information Power: Building Partnerships for Learning* overlaps and complements these efforts. Show the principal and teachers how *Information Power: Building Partnerships for Learning* helps them address their concerns.

Assess their ability to lead by answering the following questions: Do teachers and administrators view me as knowledgeable and competent? Do I project a positive and confident attitude? Am I willing to engage in power sharing and allow my colleagues to help make decisions about the library media program? And, do I have a network in place to provide me with the psychological and professional support I'll need during the change process?

Making the transition from traditional librarian to collaborative leader is not always easy, especially for individuals who view service as one of their primary functions. Keep in mind that leading is not as much concerned about the control and power of the leader, as it is about influencing people to work willingly for group goals (Brown, 1999). Successful leadership benefits from practicing respectful communication practices that foster collaborative decision making. These skills (adapted from Bill Baker, Group Dynamics, Berkeley, California) include:

Pausing: Pausing before responding or asking a question allows time for thinking and enhances dialogue, discussion, and decision making.

Paraphrasing: Using a paraphrase starter that is comfortable for you, such as "So . . ." or "If I understand what you are saying . . ." or "Are you thinking that. . . ." and following the starter with a summary of what the speaker has said assists members of any group to hear and understand each other as they formulate decisions.

Probing: Using gentle, open-ended probes or inquiries such as, "Please say more . . ." or "I'm curious about . . ." or "I'd like to hear more about . . ." increases the clarity and precision of the group's thinking.

Putting ideas on the table: Ideas are the heart of a meaningful dialogue. Label the intention of your comments. For example, "Here is one idea . . ." or "A thought I have is . . ." or "Here is a possible approach . . ."

Paying attention to self and others: Meaningful dialogue is facilitated when each group member is conscious of self and others and is aware of not only what she or he is saying but how it is said and how others are responding. This includes paying attention to learning styles when planning for, facilitating, and participating in group meetings. Being aware of body language of participants is also important.

Presuming positive intention: Assuming that others' intentions are positive promotes and facilitates meaningful dialogue and eliminates unintentional put-downs. Using positive presuppositions in speech is one manifestation of this norm.

Maintaining a balance between advocacy and inquiry: Maintaining a balance between advocating a position and inquiring about one's own and others' positions assists the group to learn from one another.

For school library media specialists who are not accustomed to acting as leaders, the idea of being proactive and visible may be unsettling. Remember, everyone has the potential and right to work as a leader. Leadership is not about position, power, or control. It is about becoming a part of the community of professional leaders who influence and empower others to foster the active, authentic learning that is vital to helping students become independent, information-literate, lifelong learners.

Information Power Team: Vehicle for Collaborative Leadership within the School

Collaborative leadership within the school is formalized in the Information Power team. The Information Power team is the vehicle that converts the energy of "people power" into resource-based practice grounded in a collaborative school culture. Working within the framework of the components of *Information Power: Building Partnerships for Learning,* the Information Power team focuses on tailoring the school library media program to the individual circumstances of their school.

The Information Power team is responsible for modeling collaborative practice and for moving the *Information Power: Building Partnerships for Learning* vision forward in the school. In assuming stewardship for each component of *Information Power: Building Partnerships for Learning,* the team serves as the "keeper of the vision," articulating how that vision translates into practice in their school. The team connects the components of *Information Power: Building Partnerships for Learning* to instructional and administrative changes taking place in the school and articulates how the components overlap and complement these current efforts. The team also arranges staff development efforts in the school and reaches out to communicate expectations regarding collaborative planning, collection and curriculum mapping,

---

LIBRARY POWER LESSON

Experienced Library Power practitioners offer six tips for making new roles and relationships more manageable: Have a positive attitude and expect new practices to work. Keep flexibility in the forefront. Know when to bend a rule, change a policy, or try a new procedure. Be patient and keep your sense of humor. Take time to remind yourself and others that the implementation of the components of *Information Power: Building Partnerships for Learning* and the *Information Literacy Standards for Student Learning* means richer student learning.

flexible scheduling, professional development, and refurbishing.

Forming an Information Power Team

The process of forming school Information Power teams may vary from school to school. For example, in schools where school-based planning or management teams already exist, there may be a committee that is hospitable to leading the implementation of *Information Power: Building Partnerships for Learning*. In other schools, the Information Power team may be the school's first effort in shared leadership.

The makeup of the leadership team will vary depending on the needs of the school community. The most effective team need not be large, but it should include:

- The school library media specialist,
- The technology coordinator, if there is one,
- The principal or key administrator responsible for instruction in the school,
- Key teachers (one teacher from each grade at the elementary level and each discipline at the secondary level), and
- Students and parents.

The Principal's Role

The principal is critical to the successful implementation of *Information Power: Building Partnerships for Learning*. The principal works with the school library media specialist and teachers to set the course for the implementation of *Information Power: Building Partnerships for Learning* in the school. Over the course of planning and implementing *Information Power: Building Partnerships for Learning*, the principal:

> Supports hiring a full-time certified school library media specialist as essential to the successful implementation of *Information Power: Building Partnerships for Learning*, and the additional hiring of a full-time library assistant as optimal.

> **LIBRARY POWER LESSON**
>
> *When forming an Information Power team, aim for membership size that is neither so small that it has little impact, nor so large that it risks becoming unmanageable.* Library Power veterans suggest that a team of five to ten people can work together effectively and also accommodate a variety of perspectives.

> Communicates norms that support the school library media program as the center of school-wide learning. The principal lets the faculty and parents know that the library media center will no longer serve as a quiet retreat for faculty, a place for "time out" or in-school suspension, or storage space for old equipment or materials; nor will access represent a privilege limited to students who are "ready for thinking skills" or "gifted."

> Provides an environment that encourages risk taking for improved instruction. The principal communicates the assumption that new practice inevitably involves some mistakes and establishes routines that allow faculty to reflect on how things are going and to learn from those mistakes.

> Advocates for *Information Power: Building Partnerships for Learning*, articulates the relationship of *Information Power: Building Partnerships for Learning* to resource-based learning, shows teachers how the principles of *Information Power: Building Partnerships for Learning* help them address concerns they have about standards, student achievement, and accountability, and establishes a climate of reform that allows teachers to implement *Information Power: Building Partnerships for Learning* as part of other instructional changes.

Although *Information Power: Building Partnerships for Learning* can take hold without strong leadership from the principal, when the principal does take the steps necessary to nurture a collaborative professional culture centered in a new vision of student learning, *Information Power: Building Partnerships for Learning* practices can flourish.

The Technology Coordinator as Information Power Partner

Information Power: Building Partnerships for Learning identifies technology as an important aspect of the school library media program and designates the school library media specialist as the primary leader in the school's use of all kinds of technologies—both instructional and informational—to enhance learning. The technology coordinator is charged with the responsibility of creating the information infrastructure and keeping it current, updated, and operational. Both the school library media specialist and the technology coordinator are vital to the successful integration of technology into teaching and learning. Together they work with the learning community to plan, design, implement, and continually refine an effective, student-centered technology plan.

As a member of the Information Power team, the technology coordinator:

- Provides expertise on essential elements of the information infrastructure and on the operation of the devices that deliver information.
- Works with the school library media specialist to ensure that student learning drives technology selection.
- Guides and assists staff with the use of technology.
- Works with the school library media specialist to plan and deliver professional development in information technology.

Teachers as Information Power Leaders

Along with the school library media specialist, technology coordinator, and principal, teachers have a key leadership role to play as leaders in the Information-Powered school. Teacher leaders on Information Power teams help other teachers become more comfortable collaborating with the school library media specialist and their teacher-colleagues to develop resource-rich teaching and learning for information literacy. To this end, teachers:

- Schedule collaborative planning time with the school library media specialist and share collaboratively developed curriculum units with others.
- Incorporate school library media center resources and the *Information Literacy Standards for Student Learning* into instruction.

LIBRARY POWER LESSON

Your principal may be the library media program's strongest advocate. Spend time educating your principal about *Information Power: Building Partnerships for Learning* and how it supports student learning. Communicate regularly about program plans, activities, and accomplishments. Invite your principal to attend professional meetings and conferences, such as the American Association of School Librarians' Conference, to learn more about the benefits of an effective school library media program, or to share your school's story.

Work with the school library media specialist to develop a system that ensures that all students have an opportunity to visit the school library media center to check out materials, browse, and use electronic resources and other media at least once a week.

- Model new practices for colleagues.
- Display student work that illustrates the results of collaboratively planned units.

Students and Parents as Information Power Advocates

Information Power teams also benefit from involving students, especially from the higher grades, and parents. A team that combines school staff with student and parent representatives maximizes the potential for "buy-in" and ownership of the school library media center as the educational hub of the school. Increasing the number of informed messengers who can spread the word that the school library media program is central to learning also increases the base of support for change.

Once involved, parent members may become the biggest promoters of the program. For example, several years ago in Denver the schools faced a budget crisis. When decision-making teams at the schools were provided with a list of possible cuts, including the elimination of the school library media specialist, a parent member of the Library Power team at Baker Middle School said, "I don't have any idea what we are going to cut, but I know that we are not going to cut the library media program."

The Change Process

Implementing change is difficult and schools often find themselves overwhelmed by the magnitude and complexity of the process. It is important for the Information Power team to take stock of how well the conditions in the school will support the implementation of *Information Power: Building Partnerships for Learning*. Any school can assess existing assets and needs using the readiness check-list in Table 2.1. Using the findings as the basis for planning, they can determine the steps needed to be able to move items from the "Needs attention" to the "Yes" column.

Initiating the Change Process

The first task of the Information Power team is to communicate with the whole faculty about the vision. As standard-bearers for the vision, leaders

TABLE 2.1

Information Power: Building Partnerships for Learning Readiness Checklist

	Yes	In Progress	Needs Attention
1. Our school has a full-time certified school library media specialist.			
2. Our school has flexible access.			
3. Our school allows for professional development during the school day.			
4. We see ourselves as a learning community.			
5. We have at least part-time support staff for our school library media center.			
6. Our school library media specialist has time to work with the Information Power team to develop understanding of *Information Power: Building Partnerships for Learning* principles and the *Information Literacy Standards for Student Learning*.			
7. We have released our school library media specialist from cafeteria, bus, hallway, and study hall monitoring and other extra or "fill-in" duties.			
8. We have identified volunteers who are enthusiastic about working with the school library media specialist to make our school library media program a success.			
9. We have put aside regular time in our daily schedule for teacher teams to meet together with the school library media specialist.			
10. Most of our faculty understands the philosophy and purpose of *Information Power: Building Partnerships for Learning* and recognizes the importance of information literacy for student learning.			
11. As a whole school faculty, we have a good understanding of how each of us can contribute to the successful implementation of *Information Power: Building Partnerships for Learning* and the *Information Literacy Standards for Student Learning*.			
12. We are ready to incorporate information literacy into our professional development routines.			
13. Our Information Power team has a small budget for extra projects that benefit learning in the school through the school library media program.			
14. Our school is committed to using the data we generate from our records to help us understand our progress and improve our school library media program.			

must engage in conversations about practice not only with those who support *Information Power: Building Partnerships for Learning,* but also with those who question its purpose or practicality, directly or indirectly. Turning these questions into fruitful dialogue means being prepared to respond to normal concerns about expected changes among school staff. The next section "Preparing for Challenges: What Do You Say When . . . ?" can help prepare the team for introducing *Information Power: Building Partnerships for Learning* to the school faculty, parents, and other members of the community.

PREPARING FOR CHALLENGES: WHAT DO YOU SAY WHEN . . . ?

Effective leaders understand that changing schools is, above all, a human endeavor. For this reason, they work hard to anticipate the concerns those in their school may have about changing long-standing practice. Part of the successful implementation of *Information Power: Building Partnerships for Learning* involves anticipating the challenges that could come from a variety of quarters. Some teachers, administrators, or parents may have difficulty imagining how the implementation of *Information Power: Building Partnerships for Learning*'s vision will be worth the effort required to change. Some may have worries related to specific practices, whether weeding the collection or professional collaboration.

As you plan for change, think through how those in your school might respond to requests for the changes in practice that implementation of *Information Power: Building Partnerships for Learning* asks of school faculty. Then, drawing on your own experience and the resources in this tool kit, consider how you might respond to these challenges. For example:

WHEN THEY SAY: "What do you mean a curriculum map? We already have the district curriculum guide and our textbooks. We don't need a curriculum map!"

YOU RESPOND: _____

WHEN THEY SAY: "Oh, I used to love this geography book when I was little! We can't possibly throw this away. Don't you think our students would love these beautiful illustrations?"

YOU RESPOND: _____

WHEN THEY SAY: "There must be someone who could use these books. Why don't we see if we can find a school in some impoverished country that could use them?"

YOU RESPOND: _____

WHEN THEY SAY: "If we take all these books away, our shelves are going to look so bare! No one will ever want to come here! We won't even look like a school library media center!"

YOU RESPOND: _____

WHEN THEY SAY: "We can't have meetings after school. Our union would never stand for that!"

YOU RESPOND: _____

WHEN THEY SAY: "Our parents don't even show up for parents' open house. Why should we bother telling them about our school library media program?"

YOU RESPOND: _____

WHEN THEY SAY: "Our teachers wrote a grant to get the materials for our department, and they're going to stay in our department. We don't plan to pool what we worked so hard to get!"

YOU RESPOND: _____

WHEN THEY SAY: "Just because we have all these new resources doesn't mean we can get our kids to read 25 books a year!"

YOU RESPOND: _____

WHEN THEY SAY: "We can't possibly allow our first-graders to go to the library media center on their own. They'd never find their way back. Besides, you can't expect six- and seven-year-olds to be working on research activities."

YOU RESPOND: _____

WHEN THEY SAY: "We can't . . . "

YOU RESPOND: _____

Nurturing the Change Process

During the implementation of *Information Power: Building Partnerships for Learning,* the Information Power team must nurture professional collaboration of all kinds to help skeptical teachers begin to collaborate with the school library media specialist and each other. In particular, school leaders can draw others into the use of new materials and strategies learned through professional development. These activities should aim to help teachers no longer think of school library media specialists as "support staff," but as teachers with equal status in the decision-making process. Over time, as an increasing number of teachers engage in professional collaboration, and link collaborative planning for curriculum and instruction to other reform initiatives with a similar vision of student learning, change will accelerate.

Ongoing communication is vital to the change process. Jean Brown (1999) offers the following advice: Set up rituals that allow teachers to "show and tell." You might begin faculty meetings and grade-level meetings with "sharing good news" or establish the "Thursday Morning Shares," a half-hour Thursday morning breakfast that allows teachers to share experiences with their colleagues while at the same time receiving recognition and feedback. Use school assemblies to recognize and celebrate successes. Not only do opportunities for show and tell recognize the individuals involved, they also alert the rest of the school to *Information Power: Building Partnerships for Learning* practices, norms, and values and invite others to share in similar events. And don't forget personal notes to people expressing appreciation for special efforts. We all like a special pat on the back when it is due.

> **LIBRARY POWER LESSON**
>
> *Successful teamwork both develops from and contributes to a school culture that honors collaboration and sharing of knowledge and skills.* Prepare the soil for stronger collaborative practice by taking some time to assess how your school's schedule can encourage collaboration among teachers and school library media specialists. Recognize teamwork. Use faculty meeting time for study groups to encourage discussion among teachers about new practices that encourage collaboration and build community (see Chapter 3 for suggestions about promoting stronger collaborative practice).

Sustaining the Change Process

Sustaining *Information Power: Building Partnerships for Learning*'s vision benefits from the work the Information Power team does to establish a process for continuous change and a culture for problem solving and critical reflection on practice. Denver's Library Power project designed a "Library Power Project Evaluation Interview" that teams can adapt to generate discussion about *Information Power: Building Partnerships for Learning*. Used on a regular basis, this protocol allows teams to reflect on successes of *Information Power: Building Partnerships for Learning* and to suggest improvements.

THE LIBRARY MEDIA PROGRAM EVALUATION INTERVIEW

The following questions are designed to be used in group discussion with the Information Power team. These questions, which are divided into three categories, should be used at the beginning of the planning process and during implementation.

Category I

Questions related to the roles, responsibilities, and activities of the school library media specialist, teachers, principal, students, parents, and other community members:

> What are the three most important roles for the school library media specialist in our school?
>
> In what ways do teachers and the school library media specialist work together successfully at this time?
>
> If someone were to ask ten parents in the school community to describe the role of the school library media specialist and school library media center, how do you imagine most would respond?
>
> When and where does planning between the school library media specialist and teachers occur?

Category 2

Questions related to specific learning opportunities for children:

> What are the two or three most exciting and creative learning opportunities occurring for children right now in our school?
>
> Describe who was involved in planning the activities described above.

Where did each of these take place?

> For each of these activities, how do staff assess and report students' progress?

Category 3

Questions related to reform and staff development efforts currently under way in your school. How can/should the components of *Information Power: Building Partnerships for Learning* enhance and integrate with these efforts? Consider a typical two-week period in the life of your school:

> On what three types of activities does the school library media specialist spend most of his or her time?
>
> What are the most frequent topics of conversation —focused on learning content and process— between teachers and the school library media specialist? Students and the school library media specialist? Parents and the school library media specialist? The principal and the school library media specialist?

Library Advisory Committee: Vehicle for Leadership within the Community

While the Information Power team works within the school to implement the various components of *Information Power: Building Partnerships for Learning,* the library advisory committee works with the broader community. Working in the "neutral space" between the formal structure of the school board and any single community-based organization, the committee wields significant power by drawing on the status of community members and the respect the community accords them. The library advisory committee includes community and school representatives who advocate within the school district and community for policies that support *Information Power: Building Partnerships for Learning*'s goals.

The library advisory committee:

> Establishes continuity and stability for *Information Power: Building Partnerships for Learning* and acts as the standard-bearer for the vision. In this role, the committee, in the words of Margaret Loghry, Tucson's library media coordinator, remains steadfast in "negotiating the nonnegotiables," even in the face of changing circumstances—a new principal, a new

contract schedule, new teachers, or a new school library media specialist.

Leverages outside support for inside change. The library advisory committee offers assistance to key players *within* the school to work on behalf of the school library media program. Community supporters reinforce changes "insiders" seek by developing a reservoir of public support that decision makers will find hard to ignore. Working together on the committee, members can build relationships that support an "inside/outside" or "top down/bottom up" strategy for change.

Promotes culturally appropriate connections with the community. Community participation in Information-Powered schools helps educators better understand how the school library media program fits into the broad spectrum of community literacy services. Broad-based participation promotes greater support for school library media programs.

Frees up professionals to reject stereotypes and support *Information Power: Building Partnerships for Learning.* As community members and professional school library media specialists come together on library advisory committees, they develop a shared vision that rejects the stereotype of "Marian the librarian." Working together, they learn that school library media specialists are teachers, staff developers, and information specialists, not the book-pushers of "the old days."

Provides a vehicle to bring community expertise to the schools. Principals, teachers, and school library media specialists need multiple kinds of assistance to implement and sustain changes. Schools must become self-sufficient in writing grants, using volunteers, developing new projects, and communicating with the community. The library advisory committee helps schools identify their needs and matches these needs with community expertise.

> ### LIBRARY POWER LESSON
>
> *Seek a balance of representatives on your library advisory committee.* Include both current and potential allies on the committee and seek a balance between school personnel and community members. Review the balance of members any time you add new members. Include at least one member of the Information Power team on the advisory committee. Either a community member or someone from the school can chair the committee.

Recruiting Partners for Your Library Advisory Committee

The library advisory committee includes school personnel, parents, representatives from community-based organizations, public and university libraries, businesses, and other interested community members. In Lincoln, Nebraska, fully 65 percent of the membership of the advisory committee came from the community.

As you form your library advisory committee, work toward a membership that combines all the skills, authority, expertise, and values that can advance the goals of *Information Power: Building Partnerships for Learning* in your community. Make a list of those in your district who have some inherent interest in supporting school library media programs. Then, for each of these "stakeholders," identify the assets and liabilities each brings to the group. Table 2.2 shows how, once you take some time to think through all potential advisory committee members in this way, the list you create will guide you in recruiting advisory committee members. Based on your analysis, you might decide, for example, that a library advisory committee that includes the principal, school library media specialist, two members of the parent organization, one teacher representative, the district curriculum coordinator, the executive director of the local education fund, the director of the local public library, a member of the chamber of commerce, and a representative from the teachers' union works best for your community.

The National Library Power Program demonstrated that generally schools need help from beyond their own walls if they are to succeed in implementing innovative practices such as *Information Power: Building Partnerships for Learning.* In establishing a strong library advisory committee, you are laying the groundwork for a network of community allies and advocates who not only can help launch *Information Power: Building Partnerships for Learning*, but also can work over time to help you sustain a strong library

TABLE 2.2

Building Your Library Advisory Committee

Stakeholders	Assets they bring . . .	But keep in mind . . .
District-level library media coordinator	Some executive authority, may hold budgetary or personnel authority	Must be "on board"; can either be a leader for change in practice and/ or may represent status quo and resist change
School library media specialist	Linchpin: offers a "reality check" for new ideas; knowledge of information literacy; knowledge of resources	Must want change and be willing to assume leadership
Principal	Key player in implementing *Information Power*	Others must respect him or her
Teacher(s)	Daily contact with the children in schools—and sometimes their colleagues	Find teachers who are willing to articulate the perceived barriers to *Information Power* practices
Parent(s)	Knowledge of the barriers to literacy through personal experience	Be sure to include all target groups.
Business representatives	Political and community support; financial support and resource networks; marketing, strategic planning and public relations skills	Owners of small businesses (like local bookstores) may have limited time, but deep commitment. Corporate members represent corporate, not personal interests; to stay engaged, they need short-term, high visibility projects that credit their contribution.
Public library director	Leadership of "the people's university"	If the public library system is effective and respected, the director can provide multiple resources and extended net works.
University or college of library and information studies	Expertise in library and information science; experience with exemplary programs	Strong source for professional development, evaluation, and student interns. May be impatient with school district barriers.
Community-based organization executive director(s)	Knowledge of community issues, experience in advocacy, strategic planning, literacy programs, and coordinating volunteers	May be competing for funds or focus. If education-focused, like a local education fund, may be able to lead the effort.
Foundation officer(s)	Knowledge of financial resources and wealthy individuals; may have program expertise	Funding may be committed to other projects for extended periods of time. You may need to get educated and wait to get on the agenda.

media program. Chapters 10 and 11 discuss the work of the library advisory committee in more detail.

Summing Up

The process of initiating, nurturing, and sustaining such a complex vision as the one articulated in *Information Power: Building Partnerships for Learning* cannot depend on any one person at the school level, one person at the district level, or even a partnership of individuals. To the contrary, success requires a collaborative model in which a variety of participants, each acting responsibly in their own roles, assume shared leadership for promoting an agenda that aims to realize the common vision for student learning that *Information Power: Building Partnerships for Learning* represents.

Featured Resources for Further Information

American Association of School Librarians. 2000. *AASL Principal's Manual Brochure*. Chicago: AASL.

American Association of School Librarians. 1999. A Planning Guide for Information Power: Building Partnerships for Learning. Chicago: AASL.

Brown, Jean. 1999. Leadership for school improvement. In K. Haycock (ed.), *Foundations for Effective School Library Media Programs*. Englewood, Colo.: Libraries Unlimited, 27–40.

Hartzell, Gary N. 1994. *Building Influence for the School Librarian*. Worthington, Ohio: Linworth Publishing.

Herrin, Barbara. 1993. Leading from the middle. *Library Power* (fall): 3.

Hughes-Hassell, Sandra. 2001. Implementing change: What school library media specialists should know. *Knowledge Quest* 29 (Jan./Feb.): 11–15.

Lambert, Linda. 1998. *Building Leadership Capacity in Schools*. Alexandria, Va.: Association for Supervision and Curriculum Development.

Nassau School Library System. 2000. *The School Library . . . Where Learning Meets the Future* (video). Massapequa Park, N.Y.: NSLS.

School Library Media Program Assessment Rubric for the Twenty-First Century. 1999. In AASL, A *Planning Guide for Information Power: Building Partnerships for Learning*. Chicago: AASL.

Web Resources

Hartzell, Gary N. 1997. The invisible school librarian: Why other educators are blind to your value (Part 1). *SLJ Online*.
   http://www.slj.com/articles/articles/19971101_5664.asp

Hartzell, Gary N. 1997. The invisible school librarian: Why other educators are blind to your value (Part 2). *SLJ Online*.
   http://www.slj.com/articles/articles/19971101_5693.asp

Public Education Network. 2000. *Library Power Resources*.
   http://www.PublicEducation.org/resources/library.htm

3 Information-Powered Professional Development

Public Education and Business Coalition, Denver, Colorado

A positive professional culture is the soil in which effective *Information Power: Building Partnerships for Learning* practices take root. It is the basis for ongoing professional learning and collegial relationships, improved teaching, and resource-rich student learning. Establishing a collegial professional culture means that teachers, principals, and school library media specialists adopt and weave together:

- New visions of effective school library media programs

- A commitment to teach all students information literacy

- Norms that support collaboration and teamwork

- Structures that enhance professional collegiality

Guiding Principle: The overarching aim of Information-Powered professional development is to develop a positive professional culture in your school and to establish a collegial community in which the school library media specialist and teachers can look to one another as resources for professional learning. Any professional development approach developed to support the implementation of *Information Power: Building Partnerships for Learning* should build skills for interdisciplinary collaboration and knowledge of information literacy. The task of planning, delivering, and evaluating professional development rests with the Information Power team, principal, and school leadership team.

Professional Development for *Information Power: Building Partnerships for Learning*

Professional development in Information-Powered schools is a powerful strategy for school change. This strategy engages practitioners in adopting new visions of teaching and learning, strengthens teachers' knowledge about information literacy, and fosters new skills in collaborative practice. The result is a mutually respectful professional culture grounded in shared goals for student learning and capable of continuous improvement in teaching and learning.

Creating a New Vision of the School Library Media Program

The Information-Powered school's professional culture draws on a common vision about the capabilities of students to learn the skills and knowledge they need to become lifelong learners. Developing a common vision for the school library media program is the first objective in successful implementation of *Information Power: Building Partnerships for Learning* practices. A shared vision stimulates interest and motivates faculty to adopt new practices.

How do you develop new visions for the school library media program if you don't know what is possible? Providing teachers and administrators with structured opportunities to observe best practices in action is the first step in coaxing practitioners to consider new possibilities for library-classroom collaboration and resource-based learning. Purposeful observations of exemplary practices can jumpstart new thinking about what school library media programs mean for student learning. Observing demonstration teaching can clarify how *Information Power: Building Partnerships for Learning* supports and influences classroom practice and other school reform initiatives. Seeing students engaged in extended research projects that result from flexible access and teacher-school library media specialist collaboration reveals more than any expert speaker or research document.

Visits to state-of-the-art school library media centers have their greatest impact when the Information Power team and other members of the learning community (teachers, administrators, and parents) have a chance to prepare for the visit, discuss what they have learned, and pose questions that arise from the visit. Library Power veterans suggest the following to make the most of such visits:

Step 1: Provide the team of visitors with a brief orientation to the school(s). Schools known for exemplary practice and schools in the process of implementing *Information Power: Building Partnerships for Learning* both have experiences to share and lessons to offer. In preparing your team for their visit, provide them with some background on the school and the extent to which the school is considered exemplary or a "work in progress."

Step 2: Introduce the "Information Power Observation Guide," located at the end of this chapter, to your team. This guide provides the team with a focus for the observation and encourages them to look critically at interactions and discourse, the environment, and the activities of students. Be sure everyone has a chance to ask questions about the guide before your visit.

Step 3: Provide every member of the observation team with a copy of the observation guide along with an "Information Power Observation Log." The log provides the team with a place to record their observations and to jot down questions that arise during the visit. A sample observation log is located at the end of this chapter.

Step 4: Set a time for follow-up discussions to focus on aspects of *Information Power: Building Partnerships for Learning* that most impress, puzzle, or worry team members.

Step 5: Use individual observation logs to structure follow-up discussions. Draft some recommendations based on those observations as a report to the larger faculty.

Step 6: Identify themes that emerge in these discussions for future professional development.

Observations and follow-up discussions are critical to building a collaborative professional culture, especially in the beginning stages of implementation. Following the visit, use the common experience of observing practice in another school or district to plant the seeds for new practice in your school. This process will begin to shape a stronger professional community and set the tone for future professional development activities.

Learning about Information Literacy

Whatever the medium, the underlying message of all professional development must be this: infor-

---

LIBRARY POWER LESSON

Make sure the delegates you send to visit other schools represent a range of professionals and partners who need to know more about exemplary school library media practices to move it ahead in your school. Principals need to become familiar with the ways in which schools turn the vision of *Information Power: Building Partnerships for Learning* into a practical reality. Teachers from different grades, disciplines, and special programs need to see that *Information Power: Building Partnerships for Learning* practices can work with all students. Be sure to include some skeptics from your staff, and don't overlook community partners, including parents and others, who can advocate for a new vision for practice in the wider community.

mation literacy—the ability to find and use information—is basic to student learning. If students are to develop information literacy skills, professional development must focus on helping practitioners deepen their understanding of information literacy. Without this "content knowledge," and opportunities to practice the skills associated with information literacy, any collaborative relationships that school library media specialists and teachers develop will stop short of the promise of richer student learning.

At the core of *Information Power: Building Partnerships for Learning*'s thrust toward teaching and learning for information literacy are the *Information Literacy Standards for Student Learning*. Outlined in the Table 3.1, the standards represent basic concepts and skills that citizens living in the Information Age will need throughout their lives.

Teaching for Information Literacy

Models that help students learn to pursue research through a systematic process provide vital content that links school library media programs and classrooms. School library media specialists, teachers, and principals who share knowledge of the research

TABLE 3.1
Information Literacy Standards for Student Learning

Information Literacy

Standard 1: The student who is information literate accesses information efficiently and effectively.

Standard 2: The student who is information literate evaluates information critically and competently.

Standard 3: The student who is information literate uses information accurately and creatively.

Independent Learning

Standard 4: The student who is an independent learner is information literate and pursues information related to personal interests.

Standard 5: The student who is an independent learner is information literate and appreciates literature and other creative expressions of information.

Standard 6: The student who is an independent learner is information literate and strives for excellence in information seeking and knowledge generation.

Social Responsibility

Standard 7: The student who contributes positively to the learning community and to society is information literate and recognizes the importance of information in a democratic society.

Standard 8: The student who contributes positively to the learning community and to society is information literate and practices ethical behavior in regard to information and information technology.

Standard 9: The student who contributes positively to the learning community and to society is information literate and participates effectively in groups to pursue and generate information.

From: American Association for School Librarians and Association for Educational Communications and Technology. 1998. *Information Literacy Standards for Student Learning*. Chicago: ALA.

process are poised to plan collaborative units that push students to reach the higher standards called for by professional associations and state curriculum frameworks.

Information Power: Building Partnerships for Learning suggests no one single way to teach students the research process. Rather, practitioners use a number of approaches, all of which help students learn information literacy skills. More important than the approach selected is that schools adopt a consistent approach across all grades based on decisions the school library media specialist and teachers in each school make after studying the alternatives. Professional study groups in your school can separately delve into the resources listed below to determine which might be most suitable for your school. Then, jigsaw fashion, the faculty as a whole can summarize the benefits of each to decide on the approach your school will adopt. The resources include:

The Big6™ Skills Information Problem-Solving Approach (Eisenberg and Berkowitz, 2000). Eisenberg and Berkowitz present information problem solving as a systematic process that involves students asking six broad questions: What is my question? How can I get my information? Where can I find this information? What can I use from this information? What can I make to show what I learned? and How will I know I did my job well? The goal of the *Big6™* is to have students approach every information problem with a systematic strategy and to think critically in finding, using, organizing, presenting, and evaluating information.

Teaching the Library Research Process (Kuhlthau, 1994). Kuhlthau provides a complete instructional program for introducing secondary school students to the research process. The "information seeking process" Kuhlthau outlines derives from what people actually do in seeking information and considers the feelings, thoughts, and actions of researchers. It includes six steps: Task initiation, task selection, prefocus exploration, focus formulation, information collection, and search closure.

The I-Search Paper (Macrorie, 1988). I-Search is a process for carrying out student-centered inquiry in heterogeneous groups. The process includes four instructional phases as students learn to: become immersed in an interdisciplinary theme, build background knowledge,

and pose I-search questions; design a search plan based on multiple sources; gather and integrate information; and produce and disseminate reports and projects. The "I-Search Unit" is the core of *Make It Happen!*—a middle grades curriculum that links subject area content, research processes, and assessment. *The Make It Happen! Manual*, available from the Education Development Center in Newton, Massachusetts, provides a district or school-based facilitator with materials that guide one or more interdisciplinary teams of teachers (language arts, social studies, science, mathematics, special education, and technology) through the *Make It Happen!* process. Materials for teachers focus on designing and implementing an inquiry-based "I-Search Unit" that integrates technology and provides visions of the kinds of activities that take place throughout the I-Search process.

Pathways to Knowledge™: Follett's Information Skills Model Kit (Pappas and Tepe, 1997). Pathways to Knowledge™ is typically used at two levels: as an informational skills model for the learner developing individual searching strategies, and as a framework for educators integrating information skills into the curriculum. As an information skills model for the learner, school library media specialists and teachers use the model to integrate information skills into the collaborative units they develop for the day-to-day curriculum. As a framework for curriculum, the model assists administrators, curriculum coordinators and curriculum/technology committees in integrating information skills across curriculum, and in changing the curriculum to meet the needs of today's learners who must develop critical thinking skills for a lifetime. The model follows no set rules. Rather it encourages students to search for information in whatever order they choose, depending on their topic and information they seek.

Brainstorms and Blueprints: Teaching Library Research as a Thinking Process (Stripling and Pitts, 1988). Stripling and Pitts suggest a ten-step research process within a framework that explains how information literacy skills build on each other. The research model involves students in reflecting on their work throughout a process that involves choosing a broad topic, pursuing an overview of the topic, narrowing the topic, developing a statement of purpose, formulating questions to guide research, planning for research and production, finding and evaluating sources, taking notes, compiling a bibliography and evaluating evidence, and finally establishing conclusions.

Information Literacy for All

In the process of learning about information literacy, your Information Power team may encounter a number of common misconceptions about the research process. For example, many teachers believe students in the early grades (K–1) are not ready to engage in research. Other teachers reserve research for the "gifted" or advanced students. Professional development must dispel these misconceptions and build support for the following three assumptions about information literacy. These assumptions ground *Information Power: Building Partnerships for Learning* and allow it to thrive.

Assumption 1

All students can learn "real" research skills at any grade level. Contemporary learning theory tells us that all learners construct knowledge through interactions with ideas, objects, and people. Students in the earliest grades in particular are accustomed to learning in this way and are eager to engage in research.

In the primary grades, students can learn, practice, and develop skills and strategies that encompass a process for approaching information, as separate from the content. Students can learn steps in the research process; teachers provide them with many opportunities to practice the process in every curriculum area. School library media specialists and teachers model and develop questions for the research, identify appropriate sources (people, places, books, nonprint materials), structure how students share the information, and provide an audience and forum for students to share their learning.

In the middle grades, students have more choice over the process, content, and products of their research. Students develop their own questions and learn to locate information sources. Students use various note-taking techniques (learning logs, flowcharts, webs, journal entries) and choose how they will share their information with others. They also begin to evaluate information for bias, reliability, and authority. The school library media specialist and teachers hold conferences with students and introduce new strategies through direct teaching, minilessons, and reteaching at the point of need.

In middle and high school, students begin to integrate the information they have gathered with what they already know. Teachers push students to draw conclusions and take sides on an issue. The school library media specialist and teachers begin to teach more sophisticated techniques that build on the basic information literacy skills learned in elementary school.

Assumption 2

All students can learn research skills regardless of their reading skills.

Emergent readers can learn that research is a means to information about topics that interest them. Students learn about asking reasonable questions and finding answers in more than one place. The focus is on fact-finding (who, what, when, where), with students working together as a group. Students gain information by listening to read alouds, looking at pictures or videos, and observing objects in the real world. The teacher and school library media specialist model each step of the research process. Students respond to two strategies— KWL charts (what I think I KNOW, what I WANT to learn, and what I LEARNED) and webbing—at this level.

Beginning readers can learn from teachers who model the research process for the whole class. However, students are now beginning to move to guided research in small groups. As students continue to develop their understanding of research as a way to find information, teachers continue to emphasize fact finding. Students continue to use KWL charts and webbing techniques. While students gain some of their information from reading, they also gain information by listening to read alouds, looking at pictures or videos, and observing objects in the real world. At this level, students begin to learn how to categorize or organize the information they have found. This enables them to share what they have learned with others.

Independent readers can move toward independently completing a research project from start to finish. When working at this level, students can read and locate necessary information on their own. As a result, school library media specialists and teachers can place more emphasis on refining the process, asking students more open-ended questions (why and how, not just who, what, when, and where) to determine if information is useful in answering their questions. They can also show students how to organize their information through additional graphic organizers. Students learn to take notes in their own words and keep a bibliography. Teachers and the school library media specialist continue to model the research process for students.

Proficient readers can move students toward topics focused on problem solving. Students can begin to use note cards to gather facts, organizing the note cards by topic. Their final projects are developed with an authentic audience in mind.

Assumption 3

Students need opportunities to learn literacy skills as part of the regular school program. Yes, children naturally ask questions and seek information, but curiosity itself is not sufficient for learning. Students need direct instruction in research skills, opportunities to practice and apply them to new situations, and time to think about and use information. What's more, students must learn these skills in conjunction with the regular classroom curriculum, not separately from their subjects. Given a research-oriented approach to instruction, most students' projects can involve the organizing of information by the end of the elementary grades. Given opportunities to learn and practice, middle and high school students' projects can involve integrating and conceptualizing information from multiple sources.

Positive shared beliefs about information literacy are part and parcel of a positive school culture. Discussions focused on the assumptions that underlie the goals and practices of *Information Power: Building Partnerships for Learning* nurture this culture. These discussions can take place in all professional development settings where school library media specialists, teachers, and principals explore topics in information literacy through scholarship and discourse.

Practicing Information Literacy Skills

As important as discussions about information literacy concepts are, equally important are the opportunities educators take for engaging in their own research. Just as teachers who write and read for themselves become more skilled teachers of writing and reading, educators who pose questions for study, gather information, and apply it to their learning are better prepared to teach the research process to their students. In the Chattanooga (Tennessee) Library Power Program, teachers and school library media specialists themselves experienced the type of learning advocated by *Information Power: Building Partnerships for Learning* firsthand. Immersing themselves in the study of such topics as the "Holocaust and Man's Inhumanity to Man," they used the very information literacy skills they would be expecting their students to use to conduct their own research and present their findings.

Higher expectations for student learning in literature, math, science, social studies, and the arts underscore the importance of teachers who know how to teach all students to use the research process to mine a variety of information resources for learning in the content areas. *Information Power: Building Partnerships for Learning* helps teachers themselves use and apply information literacy skills. Building a school community that values lifelong learning depends on teachers and students alike using information to understand the world and develop new knowledge.

Developing Skills in Collaborative Practice

A positive professional culture depends on team work. Professional collaboration and team work permeate every dimension of *Information Power: Building Partnerships for Learning*, from refurbishing to planning new curricula for information literacy. Professional development for *Information Power: Building Partnerships for Learning* must model collaboration as a program norm.

School structures that facilitate increased collaboration and collegiality are critical to fostering a positive professional culture. Opportunities for professional development must be built into the school schedule. Study groups, peer conferences, electronic discussion lists, and meetings with staff developers need to become routine. *Information Power: Building Partnerships for Learning* must be linked to other reform projects with compatible goals. Newsletters and presentations must set new expectations for teaching by highlighting exemplary library-classroom practices that promote student learning. See Chapter 4 for more information on professional collaboration.

Professional Development in Action

Given the complexity of goals, professional development for *Information Power: Building Partnerships for Learning* relies on a variety of activities to help everyone involved develop the knowledge and skills needed to create a positive professional culture and to connect teaching and learning with library resources. Professional development for *Information Power: Building Partnerships for Learning* abandons the "hit and run" model of professional development in favor of an ongoing, collegial process. Activities vary considerably depending on the stage of implementation and the type of skills and knowledge required. For example:

In the planning phase: Teachers, school library media specialists, administrators and other school staff learn about *Information Power: Building Partnerships for Learning*'s core beliefs and the practices that best support those beliefs. At this stage, visits to exemplary schools, large group presentations, small group discussions, study groups, and hands-on workshops help build a vision and develop everyone's commitment to *Information Power: Building Partnerships for Learning.*

In the implementation phase: Professional learning focuses on building professional community, increasing knowledge about information literacy, and mastering new tools such as curriculum and collection mapping. Direct instruction, hands-on workshops, mentoring, study groups, peer consultation, and coaching are some of the methods used to stimulate learning.

In the institutionalization, or sustaining the change, phase: Staff development focuses on maintaining skills, showcasing successes, and bringing new staff "into the fold."

Professional development for *Information Power: Building Partnerships for Learning* is not a one-time event. In the beginning stages, large group presentations may be the most efficient ways to introduce all staff to new expectations, knowledge, and skills. In later phases, however, teachers and school library media specialists need job-embedded learning that results when experienced practitioners engage in coaching, consulting, and troubleshooting. In particular, modeling new practice opens up teachers to "the possible" and turns rhetoric into reality. Coaching supports teachers as they begin to use practices introduced at large group presentations. Professional consultations between school library media specialist-teacher teams provide on-the-spot troubleshooting around specific problems. And study groups provide opportunities for regular, provocative discourse about new practices, such as information literacy with a technology emphasis or research with primary-level children. Scholarship and inquiry over a number of weeks allow teachers and school library media specialists to test theory in practice in a setting that promotes reflection.

If you are in a school district where several schools are implementing *Information Power: Building Partnerships for Learning*, work with school district personnel to arrange opportunities for peers in job-alike-roles to meet. Professional networking such as this encourages relationships between principals from different schools or school library media specialists throughout the district and enables mutual problem solving and information sharing across schools. For example:

In Philadelphia, school library media specialists meet monthly to review and discuss critical topics such as collaborative planning or information literacy, to set goals, and to reflect on their work. Monthly meetings provide a consistent venue for continued professional growth and build strong collegial relationships beyond the walls of the school. School library media specialists share solutions to management issues such as scheduling and space utilization, exchange collaborative units, and discuss examples of best practice.

In New Haven, Connecticut, monthly meetings with the district library media services coordinator provide opportunities for principals to share leadership dilemmas, develop criteria for assessing the quality of their schools' library media programs, and deepen their understanding of library media practices in general and their role in establishing conditions in which

Information Power: Building Partnerships for Learning practices can flourish.

In Baton Rouge, Louisiana, district library leaders have clustered schools together, identifying one school as the "lead school" for each cluster. Lead schools set up monthly meetings, rotating from school to school, so that Information Power teams can share information about topics specific to that cluster.

Developing a Professional Development Plan

How does your school begin to design its own professional development plan? Planning for professional practice begins with a clear vision for student learning and professional practice that articulates a "desired state" as different from the "existing state." Jointly developed by your Information Power team, principal, and school leadership team, this vision links professional development endeavors over time, defines the goals of professional learning, and provides direction for achieving those goals.

School-level discussions set the stage for professional development by generating a sense of urgency about student learning. As your school participates in a needs assessment process, these concerns will come to the fore and create the necessary impetus for planning.

Assessing Needs

Staff surveys that ask teachers to rate their knowledge of information literacy, collaborative planning, flexible scheduling, and related practices capture a snapshot view of what professionals want and need to know about *Information Power: Building Partnerships for Learning*. This process also alerts the staff that change is coming and communicates that they will be involved in every step along the way.

Library Power veterans recommend the following needs assessment process. Use the sample needs assessment survey from the Lincoln (Nebraska) Library Power project, found at the end of this chapter, to gather data.

Step 1: Distribute the survey to all staff members.

Step 2: Establish a date for its return; one week is usually sufficient time.

Step 3: Collect forms and tabulate the data.

Step 4: Use the data to prioritize staff development needs.

Focus groups offer a more personalized approach to gathering data. Focus groups can reach people who might not respond to a survey, draw on group dynamics to encourage responses that do not fit a survey, and profile the needs of a particular group of teachers, perhaps those who teach learning English as a second language, or those from one particular grade. Teachers engaged in one-hour discussions may contribute insight into the strengths and weaknesses of professional development and raise issues for future professional development.

Analyzing Data from the Needs Assessment

The task of analyzing needs assessment results and planning belongs jointly to your Information Power team, the school leadership team, and the principal. Careful analysis of the needs assessment data and thoughtful conversations about its meaning will result in a comprehensive staff development plan that your faculty, staff, and administrators can buy into. The plan should link the different skills staff will develop to a variety of methods for developing those skills and it should assume that staff development activities will take place over a multiyear period.

Table 3.2 shows a professional development matrix that portrays the range of activities needed to help school staff develop the skills necessary to implement Information-Powered practices.

Some schools spend the first year in a planning process, during which teams visit other schools and identify needs. The activities of the second year address the priorities identified as critical needs. For example, imagine your school's planning process identified collection development and the design of collaborative units as the most important practices needing attention. Your school's plan, then, might be similar to the one in Table 3.3.

Use the Long-Range Planning Form, located at the end of this chapter, to help identify needs in your school and to help set out the expected tasks ahead, identify resources, and identify those responsible for executing different aspects of the program.

TABLE 3.2

Information Power Professional Development Matrix: Suggested Activities, Participants, and Resources for Developing Information Power Practice

Practices Skills to Be Developed	Activities	Presenters	Potential Participants to Involve	"Tools" from Tool Kit
Refurbishing the Library Media Center (LMC) for an inviting climate and useful design	Consultation Visits to exemplary LMCs Visits to public libraries, museums, and book stores—especially children's section	Interior designers or architects SLMS Public library staff Museum staff	SLMS Library advisory committee Information Power team Teachers Principals Students Parents and community members Potential funders	Needs assessment Visitation guide Refurbishing surveys
Developing a collection that supports the curriculum	Consultation Coaching Collection mapping Study groups	District collection development specialists Higher education partner	SLMS Information Power team Library advisory committee Teachers Principal	Collection development worksheets Sample collection maps
Flexible access	Hands-on workshops Coaching Study groups	SLMS Principals Teachers	SLMS Teachers Principal Information Power team	Collaboration worksheets Collaborative unit evaluations
Collaborative planning and teaching	Coaching Hands-on workshops Visits to exemplary LMCs	Consultants SLMS Teachers Information Power team	SLMS Teachers Principal Information Power team	Collaboration worksheets Collaborative unit logs Collaborative unit evaluations
Curriculum mapping	Presentations Coaching	District curriculum specialists SLMS	SLMS Information Power team Teachers Principal	Mapping worksheets Sample curriculum maps

Practices Skills to Be Developed	Activities	Presenters	Potential Participants to Involve	"Tools" from Tool Kit
Community engagement	Consultation	Principals SLMS Consultants from public libraries, foundations, and other community organizations	SLMS Information Power team Library advisory committee Title I parent liaisons School decision-making teams Principal	Asset map Tasks and roles for volunteers Building your library advisory committee
Troubleshooting	Networking with other schools	Facilitator Electronic meeting place	SLMS Information Power team Library advisory committee Teachers Principal	Web resources Electronic lists
Professional research and thought	School-based study teams	Facilitator Higher education partner	SLMS Information Power team Library advisory committee Teachers Principal	Information Power observation guide Focus group guidelines Library media program evaluation interview

TABLE 3.3
Sample Staff Development Plan

Elements	Activities	Timeline	Resources Needed	Responsibility	Budget
Planning Phase—Year 1					
Vision building	Visit exemplary school library Visit public library	Fall	Facilitator	Information Power team	Substitute teacher pay @ $110 each
Identifying strengths	Administer needs assessment	January	Survey	Administrator Information Power team Leadership team	Printing Time for analysis
Identifying needs	Administer needs assessment	January	Survey	Administrator Information Power team	Printing Time for analysis
Forming Information Power team	Identify key players Planning session	Fall Nov.	Facilitator meeting time	SLMS Administrator Leadership team	None
Building consensus	Hands-on workshop	Spring	Facilitator	Information Power team Administrator Leadership team	Meeting space
Implementation Phase Elements—Year 2					
Refurbishing	Visit exemplary school library Visit public library and museum	Fall	Facilitator	Information Power team	Library coverage
Collection development	Consultation	Fall	District staff	Information Power team	Materials budget
Staff development	Demonstration teaching Consultation	Ongoing	Staff developer	Information Power team Administrator	Staff developer
Assessment	Readminister needs assessment	Spring	Higher education partner	Information Power team Principal	Time for analysis of results
Outreach	Create Information Power newsletter	Ongoing	Editor	Library advisory committee	Printing and postage

Identifying Human Resources

Once you have developed a professional development plan, you can begin to identify the human resources available to help implement the plan. Professional development can be facilitated by a variety of individuals—you don't have to wait until you can afford the "expert" flown in from another part of the country. Consider, for example:

Who are the in-house curriculum specialists in the school district who can assist?

Who are the teachers with specific areas of expertise who can help?

Who are the school library media specialists in the district who can help?

What other initiatives for reform in your district can be tapped as partners?

Which organizations or individuals can provide assistance in relation to specific needs identified?

How can your community partners, including local education funds or higher education partners, assist?

Developing a Budget and Resources for Professional Development

Developing an overall budget and securing adequate resources for staff development are primarily the responsibilities of your principal and district leaders, but the Library Advisory Committee can help. A substantial investment in professional learning reflects its importance and the connection between school library media programs and schoolwide improvement. Costs can include:

- Payment for substitute teachers to allow the Information Power team to visit other schools

- Stipends to cover time for Saturday and evening meetings

- Honorarium for experts hired as presenters or consultants

- Materials costs (printing, mailing, production)

When professional development resources are not a regular feature of your school's budget, partnerships with other school programs and the community are essential. Collaborative partnerships and coalitions both within the school district and within the community allow you to capitalize on all available resources and expand the professional development opportunities available for school library media specialists and teachers. Such partnerships stretch limited funds, develop norms of collaboration, and build a community constituency for strong school library media programs. What can you do to develop partnerships that support professional development for *Information Power: Building Partnerships for Learning*?

LIBRARY POWER LESSON

Effective professional development is ongoing and takes advantage of the "teachable moment." Acting as peer coaches and consultants, teachers, school library media specialists, and principals help each other over hurdles that threaten commitment to new practices. At the heart of their discourse is the question: How will what we do affect student learning?

BUILD COALITIONS WITHIN THE DISTRICT

In particular, build partnerships with other school-based or district-based initiatives that share *Information Power: Building Partnerships for Learning*'s focus on helping students research and solve problems. Other initiatives within the school district—whether whole school reforms like Accelerated Schools or ATLAS, or curriculum reforms like Equity 2000, Pacesetter English, National Science Foundation projects, Expeditionary Learning, or Junior Great Books— should include school library media specialists. Bringing a school library media specialist's perspective to other school reform programs adds value to overall program implementation. Because school library media specialists are familiar with the overall curriculum at each grade level, they bring a valuable school-wide perspective to teachers' discussions about student learning.

In the Nashville (Tennessee) Library Power Program, the local education fund pooled funds for Library Power with those from other programs to provide a series of jointly sponsored summer workshops that blended Library Power concepts with compatible approaches to hands-on learning. Jointly developed materials highlighted active collaborative planning and teaching roles for school library media specialists. In Chattanooga (Tennessee), Library Power's goals and those of Paideia, a middle school reform effort, and the district's literacy initiatives were so well matched that the district married Library Power's professional development approaches to those of other programs, extending staff development funds to include school library media specialists.

BUILD PARTNERSHIPS WITH LOCAL EDUCATION FUNDS

The Library Advisory Committee should also explore the use of discretionary school-based funds to contract with local education funds to establish resources for professional development and ensure continuity of training over a multiyear period. Local education funds (LEFs) are community-based organizations that work to improve student achievement for all children attending public schools. A local education fund convenes key players in the community, administers innovative school programs, brokers resources, awards grants, and enhances the visibility and value of the public schools.

New York City's New Visions for Public Schools, for example, has established an ongoing fund for the professional development of school library media specialists. This creates a permanent partnership between the local education fund and New York schools, with both committed to high-quality school library practice. As part of the partnership, New Visions has also developed an online resource for school library media specialists throughout the country at http://www.newvisions.org/programs.html.

Similarly, Nashville's local education fund, the Nashville Public Education Foundation, continues to invest small amounts of money in staff development activities that involve teacher-school library media specialist teams. In addition, the Foundation works in partnership with the school district's office of library services to sponsor regularly scheduled meetings of school library media specialists, including Library Power alumni and others, to sustain opportunities for professional networking.

BUILD PARTNERSHIPS WITH LOCAL MEDIA

Organizations specializing in communications—newspapers, radio stations, and television stations—are natural partners for building school library media programs and providing professional development

---

LIBRARY POWER LESSON

Your budget is both a planning tool and a fund-raising tool. It should correspond to the needs you identify through the needs assessment process and the decisions you make about which approaches will best meet those needs. Plan to use this budget in community engagement proposals.

---

for teachers and school library media specialists. In many cities, local newspapers provide workshops for teachers who are interested in learning how to use a daily paper as a teaching tool in the classroom. Public television stations can also become players in providing quality professional development.

Through a joint effort of Kentucky Educational Television (KET) in Kentucky with Forward in the Fifth, the local education fund covering the Fifth Congressional District of Kentucky, a series of training videos were developed for Kentucky teachers and school library media specialists. The series provides in-depth information about collaboration and research. Each of the 90-minute programs can be purchased for $50 from the Professional Development Department of KET. Contact them at Kentucky Educational Television (KET), 600 Cooper Drive, Lexington, KY 40502; 1-800-432-0951.

Nashville's public television station collaborated with the Nashville Library Power Program to produce a series of eight programs, Club Write, to motivate student research and writing. The fourteen videotape programs in the series, each fifteen minutes long, target middle school students. The series (fourteen programs, including a 64-page teacher's guide and a 48-page student guide) can be purchased for $895 from: Agency for Instructional Technology, Box A, Bloomington, IN 47402; 1-800-457-4509; http://www.ait.net.

BUILD PARTNERSHIPS WITH LOCAL CULTURAL ORGANIZATIONS

Local arts associations, historical societies, and museums have specialized knowledge that can enrich professional development. Moreover, the mission of many includes helping teachers explore topics through interdisciplinary learning and making authentic research opportunities available to schools. Teaming up with their staff can enrich professional development activities at little or no cost to the school. Nashville's Library Power program, for example, teams with the Nashville Historic Commission to introduce teachers to local history through historic walking tours. A partnership with the Cheekwood Botanical Gardens supported teachers in developing science units on butterflies and flowers. These and other organizations worked with teachers to develop extensive, new grade-appropriate materials that supported activities linked directly to the curriculum. For example, the popular fictional character, Flat Stanley, travels in his books to many places students have not seen for themselves. The Tennessee Humanities Council used Flat Stanley as the hook in their printed curriculum guides and children's concert series to introduce elementary grade students to instruments in the symphony.

BUILD PARTNERSHIPS WITH PUBLIC LIBRARIES

Public libraries are obvious partners for developing strategies to address students' learning needs. For example, public libraries may fund joint professional development to:

- Discuss grade level curriculum and develop complementary materials and activities

- Share calendars to develop strategies for supporting students during periods of intense library use, such as the weeks before science and history fairs

- Create summer reading lists

- Preview new items for collection development

- Learn new research strategies using electronic media

- Identify underserved populations (new immigrant families, homeless children, students with disabilities) and develop outreach strategies to ensure they receive needed services

BUILD PARTNERSHIPS WITH COLLEGES AND UNIVERSITIES

Professors of education and library science are often eager to share research findings concerning student-centered learning and resource-based teaching with teachers and school library media specialists. Often they will facilitate workshops, institutes, and continuing education programs. College and university librarians may also be willing to offer workshops on cutting-edge electronic research strategies.

BUILD PARTNERSHIPS WITH BUSINESSES

Businesses in each community have special expertise that can enrich professional development for teachers and school library media specialists. For instance, approach companies and corporations in the computer and telecommunications industries to provide training in new technologies and expand teachers' capabilities in gaining access to information through the Internet. The Lincoln (Nebraska) Public Schools Foundation found business partners willing to underwrite technology training for 600 teachers. Human relations departments of large corporations can provide training in team building for Information Power teams, and help traditional school faculties reflect on the change process in the context of their school organizations.

Evaluating Results

Planning for professional development also involves preparing to evaluate the results of your efforts. Expect to spend some time planning for an annual review of whatever needs assessment approach you adopt. Comparing data gathered from one year to the next can document changes in professional knowledge and practice over time. In particular, survey tallies should examine the percentage of teachers who describe themselves as "experts" in the areas your professional development addressed.

Summing Up

Professional development is the vehicle for establishing collegial relationships and a community of learners in your school. Schools that work to adopt new visions of teaching and learning, strengthen teachers' knowledge about information literacy, and foster new skills in collaborative practice, make wise decisions about using library media resources and practices to improve teaching and learning. Direct skills development, coaching, consultation, and networking all support school library media specialists working in collaboration with principals and teachers to lead the effort.

Featured Resources for Further Information

American Association for School Librarians and Association for Educational Communications and Technology. 1998. *Information Literacy Standards for Student Learning*. Chicago: ALA.

American Association for School Librarians and Association for Educational Communications and

Technology. 1998. *Information Literacy Standards for Student Learning Video* (video). Chicago: ALA.

Byerly, Greg, and Carolyn S. Brodie. 1999. *Information Literacy Skills Models: Defining the Choices.* In B. K. Stripling (ed.), *Student Learning in an Information Age: Principles and Practices.* Englewood, Colo.: Libraries Unlimited, pp. 54–82.

Eisenberg, Michael B., and Robert E. Berkowitz. 1999. *Teaching Information and Technology Skills: The Big6™ in Elementary School.* Worthington, Ohio: Linworth.

Great Plains Network and American Association of School Librarians. (1997–1999). *Know It All Information Literacy Video Series* (video). Lincoln, Nebr.: GPN.

Kuhlthau, Carol Collier. 1994. *Teaching the Library Research Process.* Lanham, Md.: Scarecrow Press.

Macrorie, Ken. 1988. *The I-Search Paper.* Portsmouth, N.H.: Boynton/Cook.

Pappas, Marjorie, and Ann Tepe. 1997. *Pathways to Knowledge™: Follett's Information Skills Model Kit.* McHenry, Ill.: Follett Software.

Stripling, Barbara, and Judy Pitts. 1988. *Brainstorms and Blueprints: Teaching Library Research as a Thinking Process.* Englewood, Colo.: Libraries Unlimited.

Zorfass, Judith, and Harriet Copel. 1998. *Helping Middle School Students Become Active Researchers.* Alexandria, Va.: Association for Supervision and Curriculum Development.

Web Resources

American Association of School Librarians. 2000. *Learning through the Library.*
    http://www.ala.org/aasl/learning/

The Big6™ Skills Information Problem-Solving Approach. 2000.
    http://www.big6.com/

Pathways to Knowledge™: Follett's Information Skills Model. 2000.
    http://www.pathwaysmodel.com/

Zorfass, Judith, and Harriet Copel. (2000). *The I-Search: Guiding Students towards Relevant Research.*
    http://www.edc.org/FSC/MIH/article.html

LIBRARY POWER TOOL

Information Power Observation Guide

Interaction and Discourse—How are the people (both adults and children) listening, thinking, speaking, and responding to each other? What are the signs of active learning and teaching?

Dynamics and Participation—What kinds of thinking, talking, discussion, and problem solving occur? Note patterns of participation. Is activity focused on students, adults, or both? Who determines goals, structure, activities, and outcomes of the learning situation?

Environment—Describe the arrangement of the room. What does the school library media center feel like? How is the environment conducive to active learning? What elements are distracting?

The Depth and Quality of Student and Adult Engagement—Is this a community of learners?

Action—What are the student and adults doing within this activity? Look for examples of small group work, individual study, discussion, reading, writing, etc.

LIBRARY POWER TOOL

Information Power Observation Log

Elements	Notes	Questions
Interaction and discourse		
Dynamics and participation		
Environment		
Depth and quality of student and adult engagement		
Action		

LIBRARY POWER TOOL

Long-Range Planning Form

Elements	Activities	Timeline	Resources Needed	Responsibility	Budget
Planning Phase					
Vision building					
Identifying strengths					
Identifying needs					
Forming leadership team					
Building consensus					
Implementation Phase					
Refurbishing					
Collection development					
Staff development					
Assessment					
Outreach					

Staff Development Needs Assessment

Lincoln Library Power Program

Lincoln, Nebraska

We need your help in determining staff development topics that should be offered to support *Information Power: Building Partnerships for Learning.* By indicating your level of knowledge and interest on this survey, the Information Power team, principal, and leadership team can use the results to plan building-directed staff development offerings.

Instructions for Completing the Survey:

Listed below are 12 staff development topics and a brief description of each topic. Please assess your present level of knowledge and your level of interest in each topic. For each topic, respond by circling 1) the number that best reflects your knowledge, and 2) circling the number that best reflects your interest in the topic. Use these scales:

Level of Knowledge

  1 = No knowledge
  2 = Very little knowledge
  3 = Moderate knowledge
  4 = Considerable knowledge
  5 = Expert knowledge

Level of Interest

  1 = No interest
  2 = Very little interest
  3 = Moderate interest
  4 = High interest
  5 = Very high interest

TOPIC 1
Cooperative Planning

Teachers and school library media specialists working together as an instructional team to plan the integration of information literacy skills and the use of LMC resources throughout the curriculum.

	NONE			EXPERT	
Level of Knowledge	1	2	3	4	5

	NONE			VERY HIGH	
Level of Interest	1	2	3	4	5

TOPIC 2
Flexible Scheduling

Developing the best learning environment in a library media center by scheduling classes or small groups based on curricular needs and creating strategies for making the most of flexible schedules.

	NONE			EXPERT	
Level of Knowledge	1	2	3	4	5

	NONE			VERY HIGH	
Level of Interest	1	2	3	4	5

TOPIC 3
Information Literacy and Information Skills

Identification of information skills and where they are found in the curriculum; successful integration skills delivery through use of the library media center resources so that students learn how to effectively use facilities, materials, technology, ideas and information for lifelong learning.

	NONE			EXPERT	
Level of Knowledge	1	2	3	4	5

	NONE			VERY HIGH	
Level of Interest	1	2	3	4	5

TOPIC 4
Resource-based Instruction

Delivering instruction through the use of a variety of materials and resources by becoming familiar with the resources available, how to integrate their use, and identifying topics linked to the curriculum as well as research skills needed to be learned by students.

	NONE			EXPERT	
Level of Knowledge	1	2	3	4	5

	NONE			VERY HIGH	
Level of Interest	1	2	3	4	5

TOPIC 5

Teaching Practices for Independent Learning

Strategies for developing units of study that will promote independence in student learning and information-seeking skills, and promote teacher-guided, active learning.

	NONE				EXPERT
Level of Knowledge	1	2	3	4	5

	NONE				VERY HIGH
Level of Interest	1	2	3	4	5

TOPIC 6

Thematic Units

Identifying themes or topics through which curriculum areas can be successfully delivered using library media resources.

	NONE				EXPERT
Level of Knowledge	1	2	3	4	5

	NONE				VERY HIGH
Level of Interest	1	2	3	4	5

TOPIC 7

Instructional Design

Creating units of study and selecting a variety of resources—print and nonprint—to deliver instruction and meet learning needs of all students.

	NONE				EXPERT
Level of Knowledge	1	2	3	4	5

	NONE				VERY HIGH
Level of Interest	1	2	3	4	5

TOPIC 8

Collection Development

Evaluating library media resource collections, identifying weaknesses in the collection in terms of curricular support, planning for collection renewal, determining weeding strategies, and completing the ordering process through selection and evaluation criteria that support equity and multicultural goals of the district.

	NONE				EXPERT
Level of Knowledge	1	2	3	4	5

	NONE				VERY HIGH
Level of Interest	1	2	3	4	5

TOPIC 9

Time Management for Educators

Enhancing learning time, becoming better organized, using the time available to get the most accomplished, and establishing priorities based on outcomes.

	NONE				EXPERT
Level of Knowledge	1	2	3	4	5

	NONE				VERY HIGH
Level of Interest	1	2	3	4	5

TOPIC 10

Censorship, Intellectual Freedom, and Equitable Access

Knowing the district policy regarding materials selection, controversial issues, and requests for reconsideration, and how this relates to ensuring equal access to materials for all, with an understanding of intellectual freedom, equity, and multicultural goals.

	NONE				EXPERT
Level of Knowledge	1	2	3	4	5

	NONE				VERY HIGH
Level of Interest	1	2	3	4	5

TOPIC 11
Technology and Instruction

Learning how to strengthen information skills instruction through the use of CD-ROM, Internet, laser disc, and other multimedia applications.

	NONE			EXPERT	
Level of Knowledge	1	2	3	4	5

	NONE			VERY HIGH	
Level of Interest	1	2	3	4	5

TOPIC 12
Community Connections

Identifying ways to strengthen libraries and information services outside of the classroom by creating connections to the community and beyond, for example, through speakers, VIPS, and other cooperative ventures.

	NONE			EXPERT	
Level of Knowledge	1	2	3	4	5

	NONE			VERY HIGH	
Level of Interest	1	2	3	4	5

If there are any other staff development topics you think would benefit the understanding of Information Power in your school, please list them below.

Thank you!!!

Please return completed survey to:

4 Professional Collaboration for Information Literacy

Forward in the Fifth, Berea, Kentucky

Professional collaboration animates every aspect of the Information-Powered school. In grade-level meetings and faculty meetings, and on school-based curriculum and technology committees, teachers and school library media specialists play off one another's experiences and ideas to put the school library media program at the center of learning. Together they assess needs, design and implement teaching and learning activities, develop designs for refurbishing, map curriculum, and plan for collection development. Based on the assumption that "part of my job is to help you do your job better," the work that teachers and school library media specialists do together to implement *Information Power: Building Partnerships for Learning* builds the foundation for a positive collegial culture in each school.

Guiding Principle: Professional collaboration per se is less important than its goal: Improving teaching and learning so that students use information literacy skills to produce work that meets standards of high quality. Professional collaboration brings teachers and school library media specialists together to design learning activities that teach students the steps and criteria for effective and efficient inquiry, thus setting the stage for lifelong learning.

What Does Collaboration for Teaching and Learning Look Like?

The most vital point of collaboration occurs when teachers and the school library media specialist plan, teach, and jointly assess specific curriculum units. Yet collaboration does not look the same from one school to the next but varies according to the conditions in each school. Collaboratively planned units can range from a few days in length, several weeks, a semester, or even a year. What's more, partners in collaboration vary as well. In some schools, the school library media specialist works with a single teacher, a group of teachers from one discipline, or teachers from several disciplines. In other schools, the school library media specialist works with a grade level team, teachers from several grades, or the faculty as a whole. Depending on the school, arts, technology, special education, bilingual, and physical education teachers may be involved, as well as students and community members.

Whatever the configuration of participants, *Information Power: Building Partnerships for Learning* defines collaboration as one or more teachers and the school library media specialist working together to design experiences that shape student learning. Together they plan the goals and objectives for instruction, develop learning activities, use all available resources to help students produce work that reflects the goals they've set, and assess student work.

Levels of Collaboration

In any given school on any given day, professionals can engage in different levels of collaboration. As faculty become aware of each other's activities and move toward a stronger collegial culture, they may test the waters of collaborative practice by experimenting with more cooperative relationships and greater coordination of resources and effort. What do these different forms of practice look like?

COOPERATION

Second-grade teacher Nancy Jamieson casually drops by the library media center to inform Barbara Genereaux, the school library media specialist, that her class will begin researching sea life the following week. She asks the school library media specialist to pull specific materials from the collection and signs up for a time to bring her students to the library media center to conduct their research. Students arrive on the scheduled day, conduct their research under the direction of the teacher, and return to their classroom to complete and evaluate their projects.

Cooperation involves teachers and the school library media specialist working in a loose relationship. While they may communicate about their work, each works independently and shares information informally as needed without defining a common purpose, co-teaching, or assessing activities together. Teachers view the school library media specialist solely as a provider of resources, not as a planning or teaching partner who can offer specialized knowledge in information literacy.

COORDINATION

The faculty in an elementary school decides that all classrooms will organize learning for the spring grading period around a school wide theme of "The Rainforest." Each teacher plans activities, taking into account the interests of the students, and informs the school library media specialist of the resources needed. Ms. Genereaux, the school library media specialist, locates and distributes the resources and establishes a rotating schedule that ensures each class will have time to do research in the school library media center. Before each class begins its work, Ms. Genereaux provides a brief overview of the research process. When the unit is completed, she helps teachers set up displays in the hallways and school library media center for public viewing.

Coordination enters the realm of more formal working relationships, in which teachers and the school library media specialist have a shared understanding of goals for teaching and learning. Coordination involves more planning and more consistent communication among teachers and the school library media specialist. Teachers understand the school library media specialist as a colleague who can process requests for time in the library media center and play a minor teaching role—a role specifically oriented to research and use of school library media resources. However, they do not involve her in joint planning or assessing student work.

COLLABORATION

During one meeting with her school's first-grade teachers, Ms. Genereaux asks, "Have you ever thought of organizing your curriculum by concepts?" The question triggers a new way of thinking for Selma Riddle. Working with Ms. Genereaux, Mrs. Riddle selects birds as a broad focus for learning. She and Ms. Genereaux then meet during her planning time to develop the unit. Using the planning backwards model described by Grant Wiggins and Jay McTighe (1998), they identify the desired student outcomes, determine acceptable evidence of student learning, and plan appropriate teaching and learning experiences. Once the unit is designed, they team teach the unit. Together, they and the students generate a set of questions to pursue in their study. Then, after organizing students into small groups, Mrs. Riddle sends one group at a time to meet with Ms. Genereaux in the school library media center. Using every kind of resource available, students pursue inquiry activities that help answer the questions they have listed on topics ranging from feathers to nests to migration. When they have organized their knowledge, students return to their class to report their findings to their classmates. Following their report, the class reads and discusses a big book about birds. Over the course of the unit, the process repeats itself, until all students have had a chance to be researchers and peer teachers. Finally, Ms. Genereaux and Mrs. Riddle jointly assess the work their students have done using a rubric they have developed with students.

Collaboration involves ongoing communication between teachers and the school library media specialist about shared goals for student learning. Each understands the other's role in reaching those goals, and the teachers and the school library media specialist make plans together to achieve them. Teachers and the school library media specialist also share leadership, resources, and responsibility for student learning, including joint assessment of student work. The school library media specialist and teachers view one another as teaching partners and respect the expertise each brings to the process of collaboration.

What Are the Benefits of Collaboration?

Library Power schools learned about the benefits of professional collaboration by collaborating. They report:

Collaboration strengthens the culture of the school. Working collaboratively improves collegial relations, builds an atmosphere of camaraderie, and leads to the formation of a cohesive team committed to using the best practices available to improve student learning. Teachers and school library media specialists no longer experience feelings of isolation—shared planning decreases workload and burnout for teachers and school library media specialists alike. With each sharing responsibility for student learning, both gain renewed energy for teaching. In turn, further changes in teaching and learning are more likely to occur in schools that exhibit the purposeful relationships and tolerance for diversity that develop through collaboration.

Success in collaborative relationships leads to more collaboration. As everyone learns to share ideas without fear of rejection, more collaboration begins to occur. Modeling what collaboration can accomplish inspires students, teachers, parents, and community members to seek similar results. Displays of student work stimulate additional teachers to pursue collaboration with the school library media specialist. Finally, a more collaborative culture allows teachers, administrators, and school library media specialists to make better use of professional learning opportunities of all kinds, including those offered through other school reform initiatives.

With practice and experience, school library media specialists and teachers become instructional partners, working to help all students create work that meets higher standards. As teachers work with the school library media specialist to develop curriculum units, both come to an understanding of how they will assess student work. As they develop common criteria for grading and identify exemplars of work that will guide them and their students, they also develop a shared understanding of the quality of work students must produce and how each instructional partner can facilitate all students to do so.

With collaboration, the school library media program becomes integral to student learning. Collaboration transforms the library from a place where everyone walks on tiptoes into the heart of learning. With students coming and going as they work on collaboratively designed projects, the school library media center becomes the center of learning—a lively extension of the classroom that provides students with access to a variety of learning resources.

Students become more motivated and independent learners. In schools where the school library media specialist and teachers work collaboratively to develop information literacy skills, assignments become richer and more complex. In turn, students become more engaged with learning, take greater responsibility for their role in the learning process, and interact with other students, teachers, and the community. Assignments that develop students' understanding of concepts common across several subject areas deepen learning and trigger greater curiosity about further connections among the disciplines.

Essential Ingredients for Collaboration

Successful collaboration requires a wide range of professional skills, knowledge, and dispositions, plus school structures and resources that allow these to flourish. Skills in team work—sharing ideas, developing group goals, resolving differences of opinions, identifying strengths and weaknesses, and developing mutual trust, a cooperative spirit, and sense of interdependence—are all essential to effective collaboration. A shared understanding of resource-based teaching and learning, and how information literacy fosters critical thinking and problem solving in all disciplines, further informs the major tasks of collaboration: that is, the planning, teaching, and assessment of curriculum units.

Professional collaboration may begin with one teacher working with the school library media specialist to develop one curriculum unit. But making professional collaboration a schoolwide norm means putting in place conditions that facilitate collaborative practice. Seven ingredients help take professional collaboration beyond an occasional occurrence to a pattern that is common schoolwide. These are:

- A supportive administrator who fosters a collaborative school culture
- An initiator
- A disposition toward team work among the faculty and school library media specialist
- Professional development
- Time to collaborate
- Flexible scheduling
- Adequate resources

A Supportive Administrator Who Fosters a Collaborative School Culture

At the school level, the principal is the key to the success of collaboration. Administrators who understand and value the collaborative planning process work to create a school environment in which professional collaboration can grow. Not only do they model collegial practice, they convey in concrete ways that collaboration is a valued and expected practice among all professionals. Principals who support *Information Power: Building Partnerships for Learning*'s thrust toward collaboration use their status and authority to give teachers and the school library media specialist a nudge toward working together. For example, some principals require each teacher to participate in several collaborative projects with the school library media specialist and produce evidence of collaboration for their annual reviews. Other principals make it a point to tell teachers that they want to observe them teaching collaboratively planned units. Principals who facilitate collaboration obtain resources that allow teachers and the school library media specialist to meet together on a regular basis. And finally, they recognize the results of collaboration in public ways.

An Initiator

Someone must take the first step. Sometimes the collaborative process begins with a directive from an administrator; sometimes it begins with a conversation between two teachers in the hallway. Your Information Power team is the place to look for and support initiators who can encourage and model professional collaboration. The initiator is often the school library media specialist who builds on the relationships established in the Information Power team to pursue collaborative ventures for teaching and learning, refurbishing, curriculum mapping, and collection development.

School library media specialists "knock on doors" and personally invite teachers to the school library media center to examine new materials. To introduce teachers to resource-based learning, they seek out the independent thinkers among the teachers—those who are risk takers or who are "cut from a different cookie cutter." Initiators make a special effort to make the results of collaboration public through roundtable presentations or student performances. Once teachers see how collaboration with school library media specialists can result in better student work, many become more open to working with other teachers, and begin to assist and encourage their colleagues to work together.

School library media specialists must be ready to be leaders for curriculum planning and collaboration. As a way of thinking about the responsibilities this role demands, they should review Table 4.1. Talking with other school library media specialists, in person or electronically, about their experiences with collaboration is also helpful and can provide additional insight into the collaborative process.

School library media specialists should never underestimate the importance of diplomacy and personal communication skills in initiating and spreading collaborative practice. Classroom teachers respond more readily to the ideas of a school library media specialist who is approachable and inviting. Some teachers are always eager to try new experiences. Cherish these teachers, but don't forget to court teachers who are reluctant to collaborate. Learning about their interests and teaching styles may help you find just the right approach. Sometimes teachers would rather collaborate in a subject area in which they feel strong, but full-blown collaboration rarely emerges overnight. School library media specialists looking for ways to get started can consider the following ideas adapted from Barbara Higgins, library media specialist, South Middle School, Aurora, Colorado Public Schools (1995) and from *Power Up Your Library* (1996):

Know curricular topics from various content areas and suggest books/resources for teachers to use with these topics.

TABLE 4.1

Am I Ready to Collaborate?

A Self-Assessment Checklist for School Library Media Specialists

___ Do I have a thorough understanding of the information literacy standards for student learning?

___ Do I have a broad knowledge of my school's curriculum?

___ Am I aware of the instructional styles and skills of individual teachers in my school?

___ Do I know the students in my school—their abilities, learning styles, and interests?

___ Do I have a working knowledge of technology resources?

___ Do I know my collection—how it supports curricular objectives, how it supports the teaching strategies employed in my school, and how it meets the recreational and academic needs of students?

___ Am I willing to recognize and accept my colleagues' strengths and weaknesses?

___ Do I recognize and accept my own strengths and weaknesses?

___ Am I willing to give the time and effort it will take to reach consensus?

___ Am I willing to *really* listen to others' ideas and understand what they mean?

___ Am I willing to do my share of the work and accept responsibility toward shared goals?

___ Am I willing to step outside my comfort zone?

Connect teachers who are working on similar class projects and will benefit from sharing ideas, methods, and successful class projects.

Attend team, department, or grade-level meetings. Suggest resources, learning activities, lessons, or units of study.

Provide professional development for teachers on state standards and curriculum frameworks.

Work with small groups of students from a particular class on a research project.

Be on the lookout for ideas to suggest to teachers regarding resources in professional journals, museums, or community organizations.

Meet with teachers upon request to plan units and ask, "What would you like me to do?" and "How can I help?"

Initiate unit planning with teachers by approaching the most approachable. New teachers need friends and support and are often interested in using the ideas they developed in graduate school.

Entice teachers with possibilities for showcasing their students. Use highly motivated teachers and students as ambassadors.

Reach out to colleagues who may not routinely use library media center resources, including teachers in special or bilingual education, art, music, and consumer and family study.

Teach minilessons on information literacy components as related to specific content projects.

Involve teachers in collection development.

Recognize all teachers who work on a collaborative project.

Before posting your new schedule, check with teachers who have not signed up recently.

Start a book discussion club for teachers. Focus on children's or adult literature.

A Disposition toward Team Work among the Faculty

Traditionally, teachers and the school library media specialist have worked individually in their respective settings. Collaboration challenges the norm and asks teachers and school library media specialists to step outside their comfort zones, to take risks, and to invest time and effort in working together. It requires willingness to open classroom doors and to work as a team. Group members must feel comfortable openly discussing ideas and conveying necessary information to one another and to people outside the group.

At the core of successful collaborative practice lies a mutual respect for the expertise teachers and the school library media specialist each bring to their professional work. As outlined in Table 4.2, collaboration depends on drawing on the strengths of both.

Professional Development

Professional collaboration calls on school library media specialists and teachers alike to develop new skills. Plan to spend significant time and resources learning how to work effectively with one another, especially around planning curriculum units. The school library media specialist is often key to coaching teachers in these skills. Professional development

---

LIBRARY POWER LESSON

Don't expect every teacher to participate in or be enthusiastic about collaborative planning at first. Start small. Take baby steps. Begin by collaborating with one teacher on one unit. Modeling collaboration is crucial to helping teachers see the benefits of collaboration to them and to students. Be persistent and establish the expectation that collaboration is the way of doing business with the school library media specialist. Time and patience will pay off in the long run as collaboration becomes more natural.

---

designed to prepare school library media specialists for this new role is critical. For more information, see Chapter 3 on professional development.

Time to Collaborate

In order for collaboration to work, teachers and the school library media specialist need time in the school day to plan together. Planning interdisciplinary units, reading incentive programs, and schoolwide events requires schools to set aside blocks of time on a regular basis for planning. Grade-level teams, subject-area teams, and small learning communities need time to meet with each other and with the school library media specialist to set goals, plan activities, choose teaching strategies, and discuss assessment approaches.

Time for collaboration can be scheduled in different ways. Some schools change the ways they use existing meeting time, making the principles of *Information Power: Building Partnerships for Learning*, particularly the *Information Literacy Standards for Student Learning*, the focus of several faculty meetings. Others borrow time from the school

TABLE 4.2
School Library Media Specialist and Teacher Expertise

School Library Media Specialist Strengths	Teacher Strengths
Skills for accessing new knowledge	Knowledge of the curricular content
An understanding of the inquiry process and knowledge of the research process	Knowledge of the learning process
Knowledge of print and electronic resources	Knowledge of students
Knowledge of techniques for using technology to enhance learning	Knowledge of teaching strategies
A repertoire of successful practices with a variety of teachers, students, and technologies	A repertoire of practices with a wide variety of students

schedule. Still others add time for planning by extending the school day or year. Teachers and school library media specialists might meet for planning:

During the school day: When teacher teams have regular planning time scheduled on a daily basis, the school library media specialist may meet with each team once a week. While teachers meet together, specialists in art, music, physical education, and other areas work with the children. In some schools, principals assign substitutes to cover classes, allowing teachers regular weekly planning time to meet with each other and the school library media specialist. Other schools use substitutes in a more concentrated way, say for two days every month, allowing teachers to plan in grade-level meetings with the school library media specialist for extended two-hour time periods monthly.

Before school: In schools where planning time during the school day is unavailable, some teachers may meet with their grade level colleagues and the school library media specialist one-half hour before school begins each week, with kindergarten and first grade teachers meeting on Mondays, second grade teachers meeting on Tuesdays, and so on. The principal releases the school library media specialist from other duties such as bus duty so he or she is available every day. A light breakfast provides an added incentive for teachers to arrive early.

After school: In many schools, teachers meet after school for scheduled team meetings, with the school library media specialist meeting weekly with each team. When the school library media specialist has a focused agenda and acts as a no-frills facilitator, meetings move along productively, and food serves as a pick-me-up at the end of a long day.

On half-days: In some schools, teachers and administrators have figured out ways to bank time so teachers can meet together one half-day every two weeks. Sometimes, school officials add one half-hour a day to the school schedule for four days. On the fifth day, classes end at noon, and teachers spend the remainder of the day planning together. The administration hires substitutes and instructional assistants to provide meaningful structured activities for elementary students who are unable to go home early on those days. In middle and high schools, students are dismissed early one day per week to accommodate team meetings that include the school library media specialist.

During the summer: Summer is an ideal time for collaborative planning to take place, whether over the stretch of an uninterrupted week, or on several different days. Summer institutes in particular offer uninterrupted, unhurried time for teacher-school library media specialist teams to plan for the year ahead. The networking that takes place around the lunch table sets the stage for more formal collaboration. Funding from a variety of sources supports teacher stipends, special presentations, and group facilitators for professional learning in new curriculum areas. See Chapter 3 for more funding sources for professional development.

Flexible Access

Flexible access is critical for collaborative planning. Collaborative planning requires flexibility in the daily schedule so that teachers and the school library media specialists can plan, deliver, and assess learning activities. See Chapter 8 for details on flexible access.

Adequate Resources

Adequate resources (time, facilities, resources, and budget) must be provided to assure successful collaboration. See Chapter 11 for detailed information about developing resources for library media programs.

Collaborative Planning: How Do We Do It?

When teachers and the school library media specialist come together what happens? The amount of time spent on collaborative planning depends on the complexity of the unit and the relationship among the team members. At first, collaborative planning may take longer than planning alone. As team members become familiar with each other's manner and style, however, planning together takes less time. Developing a collaborative unit is a four-step process.

STEP 1
Planning to Plan

Collaborative planning works best when teachers and the school library media specialist engage in pre-planning. By first working individually to identify what overarching understandings are desired (what students will know) and the standards to be addressed by the unit, teachers and school library media specialists notice that the time they spend together is more productive. Library Power veterans found that it helped to use a collaborative unit planning sheet to guide the planning process. Several sample teacher-school library media specialist collaborative planning worksheets are located at the end of this chapter.

STEP 2
Planning and Developing the Unit

Planning requires time. Designing, implementing, and assessing major units may require participants to meet several times throughout the unit to discuss the instructional focus of the unit, identify a topic and essential question(s), and select standards and curriculum objectives, including information literacy standards.

Developing a unit involves deciding on performance tasks and products, designing learning and teaching activities, defining assessment criteria, writing performance descriptors, creating scoring guides, and collecting and displaying exemplars. Sharing information about available print, audiovisual, and electronic resources is critical. Consider preparing a web page or webquest for current and future use. (Remember, resources may include people, other libraries, and organizations.)

Planning and designing a unit also involves determining the responsibilities of the teacher(s) and school library media specialist, developing a timeline for completing the project, and organizing the planned learning activities. Some activities may be classroom-based, others may be library-based, and still others may take place in the community. Decide on scheduling and grouping strategies. Will the whole class need to visit the library media center?

LIBRARY POWER LESSON

Collaborating partners must know their personal limitations when discussing the responsibilities they will assume and never promise what they cannot do. Saying "no" establishes more credibility than saying "yes" and then not being able to deliver.

What about small groups of students? Individuals? A combination?

STEP 3
Implementing the Unit

When implementing a unit, adapt plans to fit the actual situation. Be flexible and include additional sessions if the work takes longer than planned or find other ways to help students complete their work. Cut back or modify activities that are just too ambitious. Be ready to locate additional resources as needed.

STEP 4
Evaluating the Unit

Evaluate the unit in a final session. With every new unit, celebrate accomplishments, but also be sure to analyze the weaknesses of the unit in light of resources available. Mistakes stimulate learning and improvement. Understanding what could have worked better and how enables the unit to be improved for a second round. Ask the following types of questions:

- What went well in the unit?
- How well did the student performance tasks and products provide evidence that students understood?
- How did the *Information Literacy Standards for Student Learning* support the inquiry process and lead to improved student performance?
- How would we modify the unit if we were to do it again?
- How well did the school library media collection support the unit?
- What did we learn from planning, developing, and implementing the unit?

Two sample evaluation forms are located at the end of this chapter. Collected over time, these evaluation forms can be used to provide data about gaps in resources and to target areas of the collection that need improvement.

Electronic Communication and Professional Collaboration

Professional educators increasingly enter into electronic conversations with colleagues within their particular discipline and across disciplines to share ideas, test ways in which theory plays out in practice, and develop further expertise. The following are treasure troves of ideas for school library media specialists and teachers pursuing collaborative practice.

Since 1995, the Appalachian Educational Laboratory, Inc. (AEL) in Charleston, West Virginia, has sponsored an electronic discussion group for educators and others interested in interdisciplinary teamed instruction (ITI). Subscribers to the ITI listserv include teachers, school library media specialists, administrators, teacher educators, and curriculum consultants that are experienced in collaborative planning, as well as educators who are beginning to explore the possibilities of cross-disciplinary and cross-grade collaboration. Consultant Doug Fleming and Rebecca Burns of AEL co-moderate the discussion. Participants pose questions, identify resources for teaching and professional development, and share experiences in thematic curriculum planning and teaching. The ITI listserv also offers a searchable archive in digest format available to anyone seeking information on particular topics related to teamed instruction. For further information, explore the website via http://www.ael.org/rel/iti/ or contact Rebecca Burns, owner and moderator of the ITI discussion list at AEL, Inc., P.O. Box 1348, Charleston, WV 25325-1348; 304-347-0400 or 800-624-9120; e-mail burnsr@ael.org.

LM_NET on the Web invites school library media specialists from around the world to share information, resources, and ideas about school library media services. Participants assist one another in solving problems, link those seeking resources to sources of information and support, and alert others to conferences and news about school library media services. School library media specialists assist colleagues with tips on how to entice teachers to plan for collaborative teaching, introduce flexible scheduling to a new faculty, and find resources for professional development. For further information, contact the ERIC Clearinghouse for Information and Technology at Syracuse University at http://ericir.syr.edu/lm_net.

School library media specialists who want to collaborate with teachers are often called upon to help with the technology aspects of teaching. Teachers may seek out the librarian's help in designing a web page, creating an interactive unit on a particular historical topic, or helping students evaluate websites for authority, currency, and accuracy. ICONnect at http://www.ala.org/ICONN can help. ICONnect provides online courses to educate librarians and teachers about the use of the Internet, provides examples of best instructional practices using the Internet, and offers a question-and-answer help and referral service called Kids-Connect for K–12 students. ICONnect also offers a service for families and caregivers that enables them to become more effective users of Internet resources for youth. ICONnect is a Technology Initiative of the American Association of School Librarians.

> **LIBRARY POWER LESSON**
>
> *Create a collaboration log using a three-ring binder.* The collaboration log will contain summary sheets for each resource-based collaborative teaching unit that was planned and carried out in the school library media center. Over time, the notebook, organized by grade level or curricular theme, will become a valuable log of learning activities for evaluation and analysis. It will also serve as a way for teachers to connect with each other and build on each other's work.

Summing Up

Collaboration requires active, genuine effort and commitment by all members of the school community. It requires individuals to take on new roles, share resources, give up sole control over their students, and accept joint responsibility for student learning. Collaboration takes time and energy, but the pay off is richer, more connected teaching and learning. When teachers and the school library media specialists gather around a table in the school library media center to discuss an upcoming unit of study, plan instruction over the next several weeks, and define their shared teaching responsibilities, at the heart of all of this is the question: How will what we do affect student learning?

Featured Resources for Further Information

American Association of School Library Media Specialists and the Association for Educational Communications and Technology. 1998. *Information Literacy Standards for Student Learning.* Chicago: ALA.

Great Plains Network and American Association of School Librarians. *Know It All Information Literacy Video Series* (video). Lincoln, Nebr.: GPN.

Grover, Robert. 1996. *Collaboration: From the Lessons Learned Series.* Chicago: AASL.

Harris, Douglas E., and Judy F. Carr. 1996. *How to Use Standards in the Classroom.* Alexandria, Va.: Association for Supervision and Curriculum Development.

Peterson, Donna L. 2000. Collaboration in teaching and learning. In B. K. Stripling (ed.), *Student Learning in an Information Age: Principles and Practices.* Englewood, Colo.: Libraries Unlimited, 133–162.

Seidel, Kent (ed.). 2000. *Assessing School Learning: A Practical Guide.* Cincinnati, Ohio: Alliance for Curriculum Reform.

Wiggins, Grant, and Jay McTighe. 1998. *Understanding by Design.* Alexandria, Va.: Association for Supervision and Curriculum Development.

Web Resources

American Association of School Librarians. *Resource Guides for School Library Media Programs.* (2000). http://www.ala.org/aasl/resources

American Association of School Librarians. (1997–1999). Best Practices. *Learning through the Library.* http: www.ala.org/aasl/learning/practices.html

Wiggins, Grant, and Jay McTighe. 1998. *Understanding by Design.* ASCD. http://ubd.ascd.org/

LIBRARY POWER TOOL

Teacher/School Library Media Specialist Collaborative Planning Worksheet

Content Area _____   Unit of Study _____

Teacher/Grade Level _____   Class Size _____

Timeline _____

Classroom unit objectives/information literacy skills

_____

_____

_____

Prerequisite skills _____

Responsibilities

Classroom Teacher	*Student*	*Library Media Specialist*

Instructional strategies, including grouping of students _____

Resources/technologies _____

Evaluation of student learning _____

LIBRARY POWER TOOL

Teacher/School Library Media Specialist Collaborative Unit Planning

Teacher/Team _____

Unit of Study _____   Content Area _____

Standards Addressed _____

_____

Goals and objectives of unit (What do you want your students to know?) Include *Information Literacy Standards for Student Learning.*	Proposed learning activities and projects (What do you want your students to be able to do?)
Instructional Strategies	Resources
Responsibilities: Teacher(s)	Responsibilities: School library media specialist
Planning times	Library Media Center time needed

LIBRARY POWER TOOL

Collaboration Guide

This graphic organizer can be used by staff developers and school library media specialists to guide the collaborative planning process. Teachers often come to the planning session knowing the subject matter they want to study, for example, the human body, or the product they want, for example, "My kids need to write a research paper." This organizer makes sure that all aspects of collaboration are addressed:

Content Standards—Students need to understand the content being addressed.

Assessment—Will there be a test? Is there a rubric for the project? etc.

Student Products—Does it have to be a traditional research paper or is a multimedia presentation acceptable?

Collaborator's Responsibilities—What activities will the teacher direct? For what is the library media specialist responsible?

Lifelong Learning—The center of the graphic presents the question, is there a lifelong learning benefit to this project? If there is no lifelong learning benefit to the project, why do it?

Higher-Order Thinking—Connecting Content and Products is a reminder to include higher-order thinking skills. We need to have students work above the level of gathering facts, so that they will actually produce new knowledge.

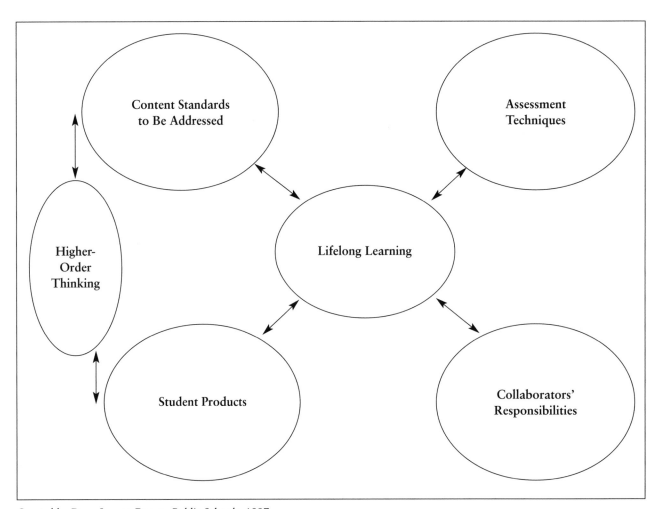

Created by Dave Sanger, Denver Public Schools, 1997

LIBRARY POWER TOOL

Collaboration Request Form

Collaboration. . . .

Teacher _____

. . . let's work together!!!!

Submitted _____

Let's talk!

I would like to talk about a unit/activity/idea . . . _____

I am available to meet with you at the following time(s): _____

At the end of this unit, I want my students to know and be able to . . . (list standards, assessment)

Let's Meet!

_____

_____

I could really use help with . . .

_____ planning activities and performance tasks

_____ getting together a classroom collection on _____

_____ creating a Web page or Web quest on _____

_____ reserving computers in the library for my students to . . .

    ___ word process   ___ Internet research

    ___ Encyclopedia or other CD-ROM

    ___ Infotrac/magazine search

    ___ Other _____

I need to send small groups to the library to work on. . . . (list topic/dates/times) _____

_____

Return to my mailbox . . . I will arrange a date/time to meet with you!

Created by Janet Malloy, School District of Philadelphia, 1997

LIBRARY POWER TOOL

Teacher/School Library Media Specialist Collaborative Unit Evaluation

Teacher/Team _____   Content Area _____

Unit of Study _____   Standards Addressed _____

Log of Instructional Activities Carried Out by **School Library Media Specialist and Teacher(s)**
What worked well in the unit?
Suggestions for improvement
What information literacy skills were integrated into the unit?
How well did the library media collections respond to the unit objectives?   _____ diversity of formats _____ technology _____ relevance of collection to unit needs (topics) _____ relevance of collection to student needs (levels)
What materials/technology will we need if we repeat this unit?

Scale:
5 = excellent
4 = above average
3 = average
2 = below average
1 = poor

LIBRARY POWER TOOL

Collaborative Unit Evaluation Form

Unit Title _____ Date _____

Grade Level _____

Emphasis Collection Area Used _____

1. What worked well in the unit?

2. Suggestions for improvement:

3. What information literacy skills were integrated into the unit?

4. How well did the library media center collection respond to the unit objectives?

5. What resources would we need if we repeat this unit again?

Use the quality rating system for the collection map.

Categories:　　　_____ diversity of formats (books, audiovisual, electronic)

　　　　　　　　_____ age of materials (up-to-date?)

　　　　　　　　_____ relevance of collection to unit needs

　　　　　　　　_____ duplication (enough materials per student)

　　　　　　　　_____ reading/viewing/listening levels meet needs of students

TOTAL RATING _____

Scale:
5 = exemplary
4 = superior
3 = good
2 = fair
1 = poor

5 Collection Mapping: One Step in the Collection Development Process

APPLE Corps, Atlanta, Georgia

nformation Power: Building Partnerships for Learning rests on the belief that school library media collections must open doors to a full range of information resources, offer information in a variety of formats, and extend beyond the school library media center's four walls to include resources accessible through local and wide area networks, satellite and cable, and interlibrary loan. The quality of the collections should challenge students, enable them to reach ambitious learning goals, and prepare them for lifelong learning in a multicultural society. Taken together, the school library media collections should support a wide range of teaching practices and reflect current scholarship in the subject areas.

> **Guiding Principle:** School library media collections are developed in close collaboration with teachers, students, staff, and other members of the learning community. They reflect the developmental, cultural, and learning needs of all students and promote active, authentic learning by providing a variety of resources for linking information literacy with curricular objectives.

Building the Library Media Collection

Developing a current, comprehensive, high-quality school library media collection is not easy.

Historically, school library media specialists built general collections to cover each category of the Dewey Decimal System. While school library media specialists considered the curriculum and the students, the main goal was to collect "the best" resources "just in case" they might be needed. *Information Power: Building Partnerships for Learning* asks school library media specialists to re-think the process and to work collaboratively with teachers, staff, students, and other members of the learning community to develop state-of-the-art collections that support the curriculum in each school, while also meeting the developmental, cultural, and learning needs of all students. The goal of collection development is to collect "the most appropriate" resources "just in time." To do this, school library media specialists, teachers, and staff must have:

- A broad view of the curriculum,
- An understanding of the implications of learning theory on collection and access decisions,
- Knowledge of learner characteristics,
- Knowledge of national, state and local standards,
- Knowledge of traditional and electronic resources, and
- An understanding of the strengths and weaknesses of the current collection.

This chapter is designed to help the Information Power team assess the current school library media collection. It provides a step-by-step guide for creating collection maps—tools developed by David Loertscher to help schools understand the strengths and weaknesses of the school library media collection. Remember, collection mapping represents only one step in the collection development process. Other data must be gathered and analyzed in order for the school to build a library media collection that both supports the curriculum and addresses the interests and needs of students. For additional information on collection development, including the importance of developing a collection development policy, consult the resources featured at the end of this chapter.

What Is Collection Mapping?

Collection mapping is the process schools use to collect, present, and organize information about the school library media center's collection of resources. A collection map lays out the breadth and depth of the collection for everyone in the school community to see. It helps the Information Power team diagnose the collection's strengths and weaknesses, hone in on areas for resource development, and track the impact of expenditures.

Benefits of Collection Mapping

The benefits of collection mapping include:

   Identify the areas of the collection that need to be built-up, stay the same, or become smaller as a result of changes in the curriculum.

LIBRARY POWER LESSON

Determining the number of resources. If your school library media collection is automated, simply query the database for the number of items in each category. If your collection is not automated, measure an inch of shelf-list cards and count the number of titles. Using this number as a guide, measure the shelf-list cards to obtain the number of items in each section. If you have a separate shelf list for nonbook resources, repeat the process, and add the number of nonbook resources to the total.

Determining the average age of resources. Expect some parts of the collection to be notably dated, especially in the 300s, 500s, 600s, 900s, biography, and reference sections. Start with these sections and average the copyright dates found on the shelf list or automated catalog database for each category. Start with 25 randomly selected items from the category. Compute the average age. Then add 10 additional items and compute again. Continue adding 10 items at a time until there is no significant difference in the average age.

Provide evidence that the school library media center collection supports the curriculum and meets the academic and recreational needs of the students.

   Show how the school library media center budget is being spent, what difference it is making, and how the collection needs to change in the future.

   Provide data that can be used with administrators, parents, district personnel, and school board members to lobby for additional funding.

   Show how the weeding plan matches curricular priorities and identifies resources that are outdated, worn out, inaccurate, or irrelevant.

Developing a Collection Map

The library media collection includes all resources available in the school library media center along with all those that students and teachers can make use of beyond the media center's four walls. In order to determine how well library media collections support the curriculum, the Information Power team should develop three kinds of collection maps:

   A *total collection map* portrays a broad picture of the current state of the collection as a whole.

   A *technology access map* depicts the extent to which teachers and students have access to technology.

   Emphasis area maps present a portrait of the current status of the collection and information about how well it matches and supports specific areas of the school curriculum.

Developing a collection map is a six-step process.

STEP 1

Collect Data on the Total Collection

Collect data on the *total collection* by estimating the number of items in each of the different Dewey categories and in specific categories such as reference and folklore. Count nonbook resources, too: CD-ROMs, online databases, computer software, videos, periodicals, and cassette recordings. Be sure to include distance resources such as telecommunication services and cooperative purchasing or lending groups. List the totals for each category on a chart. Calculate the number of items per student in each category. Add information concerning the age and quality of each collection category. Use the *total collection work form* located at the end of this chapter to record your data.

STEP 2

Collect Data on the Access Teachers and Students Have to Technology

Gather information on both the general technology (such VCRs and telephones) and the computer technology available in the school. You will also want to gather data on students' and teachers' home access to computers and the Internet. Use the sample worksheet and teacher survey tools located at the end of this chapter to gather and record technology data.

STEP 3

Collect Data on Specific Emphasis Areas of the Collection

Emphasis areas may serve large curricular subjects such as animals or specific topics such as the Civil War. Gather data on emphasis areas highlighted in your school's curriculum map. In addition, survey all the teachers in your school, asking them to identify three to five units or areas of study that they teach.

LIBRARY POWER LESSON

Quality is the most important factor to examine in your data gathering. But consider this: Quality is a measure of the usefulness and appropriateness of a resource. You cannot evaluate the quality of a collection area until teachers and students have completed a collaborative unit using those resources. Only then can you assess how useful and appropriate the collection was in supporting that unit's goals and meeting the learning needs of students. Use the *collaborative unit evaluation form* in Chapter 3 to help you assess the collection's responsiveness to student needs.

LIBRARY POWER LESSON

Collection maps are dynamic tools that help you rank the parts of the library media collection most in need of attention. Judge each segment of the current collection maps as an area to build, maintain, or de-emphasize. Add newly proposed areas to be emphasized to your current maps.

Shifts in the curriculum, standards, technology, teaching styles, and student populations mean that emphasis areas may change from year to year. Use the sample teacher surveys included at the end of this chapter to do initial data gathering and track changes in emphasis areas over time to keep your collection current. *Remember, emphasis areas may cross a number of Dewey sections.* For example, resources for a unit on Africa might be found in biographies, history, geography, art, music, and food.

STEP 4

Create Collection Maps

Develop collection maps in the form of bar graphs, diagrams, or a series of pie charts to describe for teachers, parents, and your community partners what the collection looks like now. You may want to display the collection map(s) on a bulletin board outside the school library media center for easy visibility. Figures 5.1, 5.2, and 5.3 show partially completed collection maps.

STEP 5

Analyze Collected Data

Use your collection maps to stimulate discussion about the ways you need to begin to develop your collection. For example, data in your collection maps can help you:

Evaluate whether the collection matches the curriculum of the school.

Identify areas of the collection that need to be emphasized, de-emphasized, or maintained.

Identify areas of the collection that need weeding.

Identify areas of the collection that can be supported by information resources and partnerships in the broader community.

Identify technology needs.

Identify budget priorities.

FIGURE 5.1
Total Collection Map

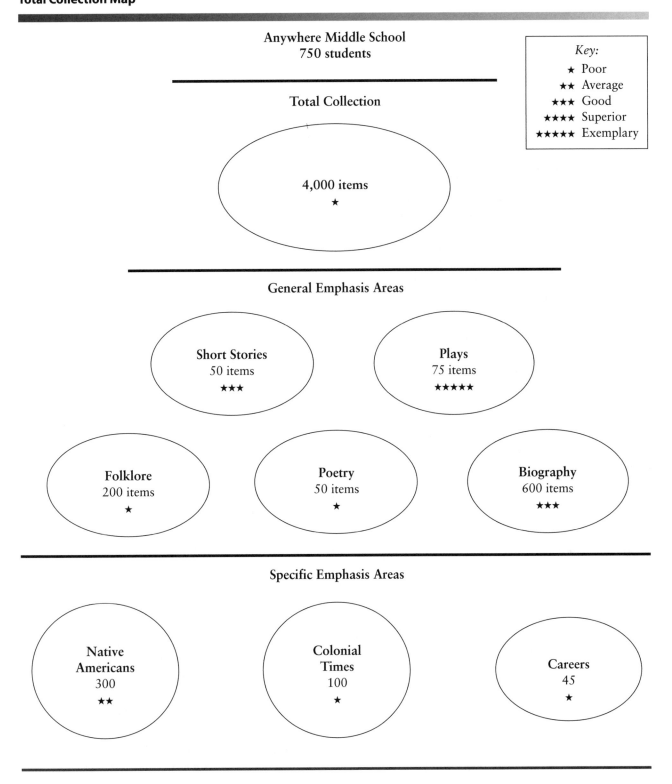

Anywhere Middle School
750 students

Total Collection

4,000 items
★

Key:
★ Poor
★★ Average
★★★ Good
★★★★ Superior
★★★★★ Exemplary

General Emphasis Areas

Short Stories
50 items
★★★

Plays
75 items
★★★★★

Folklore
200 items
★

Poetry
50 items
★

Biography
600 items
★★★

Specific Emphasis Areas

Native
Americans
300
★★

Colonial
Times
100
★

Careers
45
★

FIGURE 5.2

Emphasis Collection Map

Anywhere Elementary School
450 students

Multicultural Picture Books ★
(change in population; need more
African American and Hispanic)

Transition Novels ★
(change to Balanced Literacy; need more
for independent reading component)

Beginning-to-Read Books ★★
(change to Balanced Literacy; need more for
independent reading component)

Native Americans ★★★
(print resources adequate; need more visual resources:
CD-ROMs, videos, other electronic resources)

Key:
★ Poor
★★ Fair
★★★ Good
★★★★ Superior
★★★★★ Exemplary

FIGURE 5.3

Technology Access Collection Map

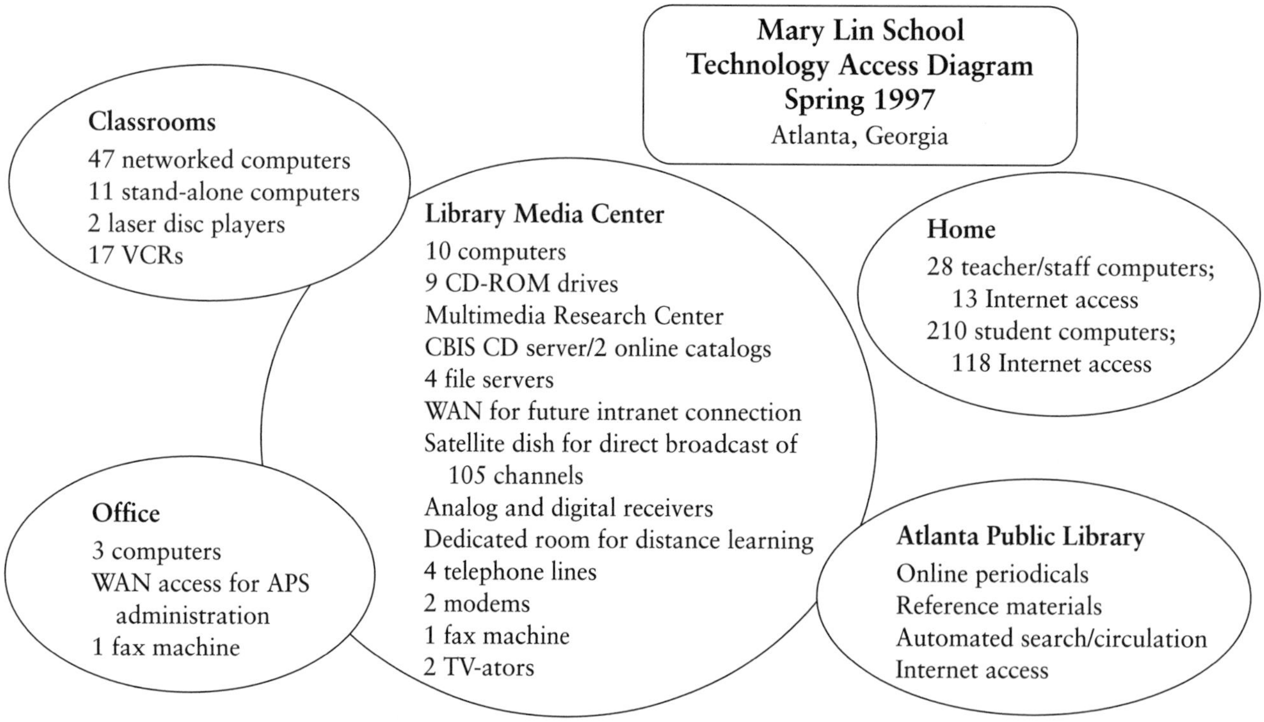

Mary Lin School
Technology Access Diagram
Spring 1997
Atlanta, Georgia

Classrooms
47 networked computers
11 stand-alone computers
2 laser disc players
17 VCRs

Library Media Center
10 computers
9 CD-ROM drives
Multimedia Research Center
CBIS CD server/2 online catalogs
4 file servers
WAN for future intranet connection
Satellite dish for direct broadcast of
    105 channels
Analog and digital receivers
Dedicated room for distance learning
4 telephone lines
2 modems
1 fax machine
2 TV-ators

Home
28 teacher/staff computers;
    13 Internet access
210 student computers;
    118 Internet access

Office
3 computers
WAN access for APS
    administration
1 fax machine

Atlanta Public Library
Online periodicals
Reference materials
Automated search/circulation
Internet access

Create Proposed Collection Maps

Proposed collection maps show collection targets for a 2–4 year period of time. They provide a picture of "where we want to go." In developing proposed collection maps, it is important to understand the current curriculum and likely curricular changes on the horizon, the normal evolution of topics taught, trends in print and electronic publishing, and changes in the student population.

To create your proposed collection maps, use your curriculum maps (see Chapter 6) to make a master list of curricular units and topics. Prioritize this list and then hold it up against each of the current collection maps (total, technology, and emphasis) to decide how the collection will need to change

---

LIBRARY POWER LESSON

Don't be surprised if some teachers, parents, and community members—even those on your Library Advisory Committee or Information Power team—consider weeding the collection an unnecessary and wasteful process. Remain firm when skeptics raise questions about weeding. Explain that a collection of out-of-date, torn, and culturally biased resources subtly tells students, "We don't care enough about you to provide the best for you." Make it clear that receiving incorrect information is harmful to children. Although not everyone will readily accept that "no information is better than misinformation," most will agree that 1950s-era books that predict the future use of computers are not useful or appropriate for today's students.

---

over the next two to four years in order to support the curriculum. Figure 5.4 shows a sample proposed collection map.

Using Collection Maps

Collection maps should be used to help your Information Power team make collection development decisions. For example, you might use the general emphasis areas of the map to develop a three-year collection development budget. In your budget, include the targeted areas, the justification for your decisions, the quantity of materials, and proposed expenditures. See Figure 5.5 for a sample budget plan.

The Information Power team can also use collection maps to suggest parts of the collections that need to be weeded. Many school library media collections, especially in disadvantaged rural

---

FIGURE 5.4
Proposed Collection Map

General Emphasis Collections	
Folklore and fairy tales	200 items
Animals	260 items

Specific Emphasis Collections	
Indians of North America	150 items
Frontier and pioneer life	200 items
Dinosaurs	60 items
Culture	200 items
China	150 items
Japan	150 items

From: Loertscher, David V., and May Lein Ho. 1996. *Collection Mapping in the LMC.* San Jose, Calif.: Hi Willow Research and Publishing.

FIGURE 5.5

Budget Plan for General Emphasis Areas

School: _____Anywhere Elementary School_____

Number of students: _____500_____

Date: _____September 1999_____

General Emphasis Areas	Justification	Year 1 Expenditure	Year 2 Expenditure	Year 3 Expenditure
Beginning-to-read	Move to balanced literacy; # of students reading below grade level high; want to go from 450 to 600 items	$500	$500	$500
Transition novels	Move to balanced literacy; # of students reading below grade level high; want to go from 200 to 300 items	$350	$350	$350
Picture books and fiction that reflect ethnic background of our students	Student population: 75% African American; 25% Latino; collection <2%	$500	$500	$500

and urban districts, have suffered over the years from a lack of funds, lack of attention from professional staff, and lack of recognition at "the top" that access to library media centers and information is essential to student learning. As a result, the library collections are inadequate to support current curriculum demands or meet the interests of today's students. In addition, many of the collections do not reflect the ethnic richness and diversity of the school community. The remedy for an outdated and tattered collection of resources, many predicting events that have long since come and gone, is deselection or weeding—removing the outmoded resources to make space for new materials that promote student learning. For detailed information on weeding, see the featured resources located at the end of this chapter.

Collection maps can also help your Information Power team identify resource needs that can best be met by joining consortia or forming partnerships with other libraries and organizations within the community. For example, in Nashville, the collection maps indicated a need for technical and scientific materials for the high schools. Nashville public schools joined Project Athena (Accessing Technological Horizons to Educate the Nashville Area), a consortium of ten area colleges and universities, the public library, and the state archives, to provide increased access for students.

Technology access maps can provide critical information about student and teacher access to technology that your Information Power team and other school leadership can use to develop the school's technology plan. See Chapter 7 for information on writing a technology plan.

Finally, use collection maps as public relations tools. Create a large poster of the maps for public display. Administrators, teachers, students, and parents will be able see that the school's library media collection has a purpose, direction, and curricular foundation. Potential funders will be able to see where additional financial support is needed. If you revise the maps as resources are added to the collections, you will be able to indicate curricular changes and new technology initiatives, and show progress to decision makers and funders.

Summing Up

Collection mapping helps the Information Power team understand the strengths and weaknesses of the current collection and represents one step in the collection development process. Chapter 6 provides step-by-step instructions on curriculum mapping—a process used to attain a clear, succinct view of the curriculum.

Featured Resources for Further Information

Emery, Francine. 1997. *That's Me! That's You! That's Us! Selected Current Multicultural Books for Children and Young Adults Presenting Positive, Empowering Images*. Philadelphia: The Multicultural Resource Center (215-438-2729).

Hughes, Sandra M., and Jacqueline C. Mancall. 1999. Developing a collaborative access environment: Meeting the resource needs of the learning community. In B. K. Stripling (ed.), *Student Learning in an Information Age: Principles and Practices*. Englewood, Colo.: Libraries Unlimited, 231–59.

Kachel, Debra. 1997. *Collection Assessment and Management for School Libraries: Preparing for Cooperative Collection Development*. Westport, Colo.: Greenwood Press.

Loertscher, David V., and May Lein Ho. 1996. *Collection Mapping in the LMC*. San Jose, Calif.: Hi Willow Research and Publishing.

Loertscher, David V., Blanche Woolls, and Janice Felker. 1998. *Building a School Library Collection Plan: A Beginning Handbook with Internet Assist*. San Jose, Calif.: Hi Willow Research and Publishing.

Web Resources

Bertland, Linda. October 5, 2000. *Collection development*. http://www.sldirectory.com/libsf/resf/coldev2.html

Cooperative Children's Book Center (CCBC) of the School of Education at the University of Wisconsin–Madison. http://www.education.wisc.edu/ccbc/

Loertscher, David V., Blanche Woolls, and Janice Felker. 1998. *Building a School Library Collection Plan: A Beginning Handbook with Internet Assist*. http://lmcsource.com/felker/index.html

LIBRARY POWER TOOL

Total Collection Work Form

School name: _____

Grade levels: _____

Number of students: _____

Record in the following table the numbers of items in each category. Do not
spend more than two hours collecting data for the table.

	LMC	Class-rooms	Total	Number/ Student	Age	Quality
Reference (general)						
Reference (encyclopedia)						
000						
100						
200						
300						
398.2						
400						
500						
590						
600						
700						
800						
900						
920						
Biography						
Easy						
Fiction						
Picture						
Periodicals						
Professional collection						
Parent collection						
Total						

Adapted from Loertscher, David V., and May Lein Ho. 1996. *Collection Mapping in the LMC.* San Jose, Calif.: Hi Willow Research and Publishing.

LIBRARY POWER TOOL

Technology Access Work Form

School: _____

Number of Students: _____

Record the numbers of items in each category.

General Technology

	LMC	Classroom	Public Library	Total
Televisions				
VCRs				
Cable connection				
Satellite connection				
Laser disc players				
CD-ROM players (music)				
Tape players				
Copy machines				
Fax machines				
Telephones				
Other				
			Total	

Computer Technology

	LMC	Classroom	Public Library	Home Students	Home Teachers	Total
Computers						
CD-ROM drives						
Internet connections						
Scanners						
Printers						
DVD drives						
					Total	

LIBRARY POWER TOOL

Emphasis Collections Work Form

Emphasis Area Analyzed: _____

Record the numbers of items in each category that support this emphasis area.
Use estimates when actual figures are not available.

	LMC	Class-rooms	Total	Number/ Student	Age	Quality
Books						
Reference						
Nonfiction						
398.2						
Biography						
Fiction						
Story collection						
Easy						
Professional						
Audiovisual materials						
Audio						
Books on tape						
Videos						
Laser discs						
Filmstrips						
Graphic						
Periodicals						
Current						
Back issues						
Full-text CD-ROM, online subscription, microform						
Electronic resources						
CD-ROM						
Online subscriptions						

Adapted from Loertscher, David V., and May Lein Ho. 1996. *Collection Mapping in the LMC*. San Jose, Calif.: Hi Willow Research and Publishing

LIBRARY POWER TOOL

Teacher Survey #1
Collecting Data about the Total Collection

In order to complete and update our collection maps and technology charts, the following information is needed no later than _____. Please return your form to the library media center or place it in my mailbox.

Teacher: _____   Grade/subject area: _____

Print Items in Your Classroom:

Sets of encyclopedias _____

Nonfiction books _____

Fiction books (include theme books): _____

Periodicals (e.g., *Weekly Reader*): count a one-year subscription of a single title as one. _____

Audiovisual Materials in Your Classroom:

Films/videos: _____   CD-ROMs (music): _____

Cassette tapes: _____   Records: _____

CD-ROMs (computer): _____   Other: _____

Technology Information:

Computers in the classroom: _____

CD-ROM drives in the classroom: _____

Number of computers in the home: _____

Student (hand count) _____; Internet (hand count) _____

Teacher/staff _____; Internet _____

Adapted from a form developed by Mary Lin Elementary School, Atlanta, Georgia

Teacher Survey #2
Survey for Collecting Data about the Emphasis Areas

Dear Staff Members,

A collection map is a visual representation of the strengths and weaknesses of a library media center collection. The development of the collection is driven by the needs of the curriculum.

    We are getting ready to purchase new materials for our collection. We need your assistance in making our selections. Please list five emphasis areas that have an impact on what you teach and which lend themselves to the use of a variety of materials across the collection.

    Definition: Emphasis areas are clumps of materials purchased to support a curricular area. There are two types: general emphasis collections (support numerous units or whole courses of instruction) and specific emphasis collections (support single topics or units).

* *

Date due: _____

Teacher's name: _____

Grade level/discipline: _____

Emphasis areas: _____

                           _____

                           _____

                           _____

                           _____

Adapted from a form developed by Price Middle School, Atlanta, Georgia

6 Curriculum Mapping

APPLE Corps, Atlanta, Georgia

Promoting student achievement of learning goals in the Information-Powered school requires teachers, administrators, and school library media specialists to develop a thorough knowledge of subject area and grade-level curricula. Teachers who work together in the same building may have only a vague idea of what goes on in one another's classrooms. Curriculum mapping draws back the curtain on the curriculum of the whole school and paints a portrait of who is teaching what, with which students in each grade level, and at what time of the calendar year. It allows schools to identify gaps and repetitions in the curriculum, target potential areas for integration, match assessment with standards, and provide the resources that teachers need for effective instruction. Curriculum mapping also communicates to students and parents the concepts and skills that students are learning in each grade and subject area.

> **Guiding Principle:** A careful and effective process of curriculum mapping takes time, thought, trust, and focused work. Creating and refining the maps are an ongoing collaborative process. The collegial professional environment developed through this collaboration sets the stage for further discussions about overlaps and gaps in the curriculum, expectations for learning, the extent to which all students have access to high quality curriculum, and ways

the school library media program supports student learning.

What Is Curriculum Mapping?

According to Heidi Hayes Jacobs, a recognized expert on curriculum mapping, curriculum mapping is a systematic process that helps school teams consolidate information from curriculum, guides, and textbooks into a clear, succinct, and visual picture of what is happening in the school (1997). The curriculum maps that result from the mapping process describe all elements of the curriculum—the content, standards, essential concepts and topics, learning processes, and skills that teachers emphasize, as well as the products and performances that represent what students have learned.

Curriculum mapping allows individual schools, and even districts, to refine their curriculum articulation and integration (Jacobs, 1997). Curriculum maps can help teachers, administrators, and school library media specialists:

Determine how state and local standards are being addressed.

Identify the "enacted" curriculum—the skills and concepts teachers choose to teach in the course of an academic year. Differences between what teachers actually teach and what the school district's curriculum guides or frameworks list as being taught become key points for discussion.

Check for continuity and determine if the curriculum is "spiraling" so that students learn key concepts in greater depth and complexity from one year to the next. For example, if the topic "magnets" appears in the curriculum map of the kindergarten, third grade, and fourth grade, that pattern should trigger discussion about the learning goals for each grade: Are students learning about different aspects of magnetism in different grades? If in kindergarten, students simply explore magnets, how does their learning in third grade extend to understanding the concepts of poles, attracting, and repelling? Then, what do students learn in fourth grade that extends their learning to the role magnets play in the production of electricity?

Identify areas of repetition and gaps in the curriculum.

Reveal the level or potential for interdisciplinary or cross-grade-level collaboration.

Communicate to parents and students which teachers are teaching which skills, content, and concepts, and also when teachers are focusing on which themes.

Curriculum mapping is particularly important to the development of an Information-Powered library media program. Curriculum mapping enables school library media specialists to:

Make connections between content learning and information literacy skills.

Collaborate with teachers to integrate information literacy competencies throughout the teaching and learning process.

Create and promote a rationale for infusing information literacy standards for student learning into curricular and instructional policies for the school.

Recommend appropriate information resources to support information literacy and critical thinking throughout the curriculum.

Creating Curriculum Maps

The step-by-step directions provided below are adapted from Jacobs' book *Mapping the Big Picture: Integrating Curriculum and Assessment K–12* (1997)

and are designed to get you started. For more detail, see the resources listed at the end of this chapter.

STEP 1

Collect Professional Material and Read Widely about Curriculum Mapping

The Information Power team and the whole faculty must become familiar with the concept of curriculum mapping, especially the benefits of curriculum mapping. Jacobs' book, *Mapping the Big Picture: Integrating Curriculum and Assessment K–12,* and the video, *Curriculum Mapping: Charting the Course of Content* (ASCD, 1999), not only provide detailed information on the curriculum mapping process but also provide compelling arguments for engaging in the process.

STEP 2

Decide on the Kind of Information You Will Gather

As Jacobs (1997) points out, it is important for the faculty to look at a number of sample curriculum maps to determine the categories to include in their maps. Professional study groups in your school can use the maps located at the end of this chapter to determine which categories will be most useful for your school. If teachers in your school are not familiar with curriculum mapping, the maps can also help them think about how curriculum maps might be used and understand the degree of detail curriculum mapping requires.

The complexity of the curriculum map your school develops will depend on the perceived needs of your faculty, the teaching and learning philosophy of the school, the school's grade organization, and the time frame you wish to analyze. At a minimum you will want to gather a brief description of the content (whether it is student-centered, interdisciplinary, or discipline-based), a description of the standards, processes and skills emphasized, and the nature of the assessment students produce as evidence of growth. You may also decide to include essential questions, the length of instruction, the primary teaching method, materials, and the organization of instruction.

STEP 3

Collect Data on the Curriculum of the School

There are a number of formats for collecting data. Several are located at the end of this chapter. Select one worksheet form for everyone in the school to use.

Entering information into a database allows for greater manipulation of the data; however, as Jacobs (1997) points out, some schools still find that writing on a large sheet of butcher block paper or standard 8½″ by 11″ sheets of paper works best for them.

Make sure teachers understand the mapping task and give them an approximate time frame for completing maps. Jacobs (1997) found that most individual elementary teachers take about one hour to complete the content portion of the map for one school year. Most secondary teachers take about 45 minutes per course per year for the content data. Completion of the skills and assessment components of the map takes longer because they involve serious reflection on the primary skills and the most important assessments. It is critical that each teacher complete his or her own calendar-based map. As Jacobs points out, the map must contain authentic data and the classroom teacher is the only one who can provide it.

Analyzing and Using Curriculum Maps

As Jacobs (1997) points out, after the curriculum maps have been compiled, the real work beings. The faculty must now analyze the maps to gain information they can use to make important curricular and resource decisions. Review the maps for:

- Gaps and repetitions in the curriculum

- Evidence of standards in practice

- Areas for potential interdisciplinary and cross-grade level collaboration

- Learning goals and skills that require students to use information literacy skills

- School library media center and classroom resource needs, including technology

- Appropriate assessments to demonstrate student learning.

LIBRARY POWER LESSON

Allow time at a faculty meeting for teachers to complete their curriculum maps. Grade-level meetings are also a good time for teachers to work on their curriculum maps. Remind teachers that highly specific information about daily lesson plans is not needed. The purpose of the map is to provide a realistic overview of what each teacher teaches in the course of the school year. If teachers are reluctant to complete curriculum maps that cover an entire year, consider developing a map that covers only one semester or term at a time.

Summing Up

Students are the prime beneficiaries of curriculum mapping. Library Power veterans found that curriculum maps expanded their perspective and increased the quality of their educational decisions. With a thorough knowledge of subject area and grade level curricula, school library media specialists were able to promote competency in information literacy across the curriculum, collaborate regularly with teachers to design and implement authentic learning activities, and provide resources that supported and enhanced the curriculum.

Featured Resources for Further Information

Eisenberg, Michael B., and Robert E. Berkowitz. 1988. *Curriculum Initiative: An Agenda and Strategy for Library Media Programs.* Norwood, N.J.: Ablex.

Curriculum Mapping: Charting the Course of Content (video). 1999. Alexandria, Va.: Association for Supervision and Curriculum Development.

Jacobs, Heidi Hayes. 2000. *Focus on Curriculum Mapping: ASCD Curriculum Handbook.* Alexandria, Va.: Association for Supervision and Curriculum Development.

Jacobs, Heidi Hayes. 1997. *Mapping the Big Picture: Integrating Curriculum and Assessment K–12.* Alexandria, Va.: Association for Supervision and Curriculum Development.

Jacobs, Heidi Hayes. 2000. Upgrading the K–12 journey through curriculum mapping: A technology tool for classroom teachers, media specialists, and administrators. *Knowledge Quest* 29 (Nov./Dec.): 25–29.

Web Resources

Jacobs, Heidi Hayes. 1997. *Mapping the Big Picture: Integrating Curriculum and Assessment K–12,* Chapters 1 and 2. Alexandria, Va.: Association for Supervision and Curriculum Development. http://www.ascd.org/readingroom/books/jacobs97book.html

LIBRARY POWER TOOL

Sample Curriculum Map

School: Chattanooga School for Liberal Arts   Grade: 4   Subject: Social Studies

	August/September	October	November	December
Essential Questions	How does the geography of a place affect the way people live? How do I read a map?	How did Tennessee's geography affect the lives of native Tennesseans? What lessons can we learn from them?	Why did settlers move to Tennessee? How did Tennessee become a state?	
Assessments	Create a map of *Morning Girl*'s island, with a legend 3.4.1, 3.4.2, 3.4.3 Written tests throughout the year on current events from "Time for Kids"	Native American flip book (group project, including topographical Tennessee map)	Pioneer research project (written report comparing pioneer life to today)	
Related Literature	*Morning Girl*	*Sign of the Beaver* or *Blue Willow* Native American legends and tales	*Jack Tales* *Dear Mr. Henshaw*	*Dear Mr. Henshaw*
Field Studies		Appalachia history museum		
Citizen-ship	Current events discussed throughout the year using "Time for Kids"			
Diversity	Examine the island culture and beliefs/relate to island environment	Identify Native American community characteristics	Identify characteristics of pioneer communities	
Geography	Identify and use geographical terms from *Morning Girl*	Relate the way native Tennesseans lived to their environment Use and conservation of natural resources		
Local, U.S. and World History		Compare the way natives used the land and the way natural resources are used today	Compare the lives of pioneers to the way we live today	
Historical Inquiry		Research and prepare reports on Native Tennesseans	Research pioneer life and prepare reports	
Economic Systems			Examine development and growth of early Tennessee settlements and cities	

High School Physics Curriculum Map (September–December)

	Content	Skills	Assessment
September	Measuring systems Uncertainties in measurement Vector addition	Make measurements in SI units Present the results of an experiment as a lab report Use a computer graphing program Add vectors using trigonometry Use significant figures in collecting and manipulating data Analyze graphs of data for slope and the equation of the line	Written lab reports Tests: problems, multiple choice, essay
October	Linear motion Vector addition Acceleration of gravity	Vector addition continued Analyze the effect of forces on motion Use algebra to solve equations for motion Represent the motion of a body as position versus time and velocity versus time graphs from lab data Determine the acceleration of gravity in the lab	Written lab reports Tests: problems, multiple choice, essay Lab performance Scientist report (library research) Oral presentation of group problem-solving activity
November	Newton's Laws of Motion Forces Torque	Add force vectors using trigonometry as well as in the lab Draw free body diagrams to isolate the forces acting on a body For a body of equilibrium, show that EA. = 0 and write equations to represent this Analyze force problems involving friction, inclines, and torques	Written lab reports Tests: problems, multiple choice, essay Lab performance Lab report written in IMRAD form
December	Motion in two dimensions Centripetal forces Gravitation	Identify real and fictitious forces Use algebra to solve sets of equations relating the vertical and horizontal components of 2D motion Describe gravitation as one of the forces of nature	Written lab reports Tests: problems, multiple choice, essay Lab performance Design problem "10m vehicle"

From: Jacobs, Heidi Hayes. 1993. *Mapping the Big Picture: Integrating Curriculum and Assessment K–12.* Alexandria, Va.: ASCD.

Sample 5th Grade Integrated Curriculum Map (September–December)

	September	October	November	December
Language Arts	*Four Ancestors* (Bruchac) Writing workshop Sentence study	Journal writing Paragraph study Writing workshop	*Sign of the Beaver* or *Calico Bush* → Genre study both reading and writing (historical fiction) Writing workshop	Writing workshop Part of speech
Social Studies	Geography Explorers Native Americans	Colonization ————————→		Revolutionary War ————————→
Science	Energy: Radiant/Geothermal Fossil fuels/nuclear Uses/problems Sources forms— kinetic/potential	————————→	Machines and motion Six simple machines	————————→
Math	Place value Mean/average Exponents Computation Problem solving	Decimals to hundredths Computation Graphing Problem solving	Probability and statistics Sample size and sampling Graphing	Interpreting data Predicting Graphing Problem solving
Art	Native American art	————————→	17th- and 18th-century American art	————————→
Music	Focus on Native American musical heritage	————————→	Early American music	Patriotic music

LIBRARY POWER TOOL

Curriculum Mapping Worksheet

Teacher _____   Grade _____   Subject _____

	Content	Skills	Assessments
September			
October			
November			
December			
January			
February			
March			
April			
May			
June			

LIBRARY POWER TOOL

Curriculum Mapping Worksheet

Date _____

Grade _____ Instructor _____ Subject _____

Unit _____

Total Periods of Instruction _____

Calendar Quarter _____

Level of Instruction _____

_____ Introduced

_____ Reinforced

_____ Expanded

Primary Teaching Method _____

_____ Desk work   _____ Programmed (includes learning stations)

_____ Lecture   _____ Project

_____ Demonstration   _____ Report

_____ Discussion   _____ Combination

_____ Independent study

Materials _____

_____ Text

_____ One source

_____ Multiple sources

Organization of Instruction _____

_____ Large group   _____ Individual

_____ Small group   _____ Combination

Evaluation _____

_____ Test   _____ Report

_____ Product   _____ Combination

_____ Observation

Comments _____

From: Eisenberg, Michael B., and Robert E. Berkowitz. 1988. *Curriculum Initiative: An Agenda and Strategy for Library Media Programs.* Norwood, N.J.: Ablex.

LIBRARY POWER TOOL
Curriculum Mapping Worksheet

Teacher _____   Grade _____   Subject _____

	Essential Questions	*Content Area(s)*	*Skills*	*Assessments*
September				
October				
November				
December				
January				
February				
March				
April				
May				
June				

7 Enhancing Student Learning with Technology

Sandra Hughes-Hassell

*I*nformation Power: Building Partnerships for *Learning* emphasizes the role of technology—both instructional and informational—in enhanced student learning and identifies the school library media specialist as a primary leader in the school's use of technology. In Information-Powered schools, school library media specialists are responsible for helping teachers use technology in innovative ways across the curriculum, designing student experiences that use technology in authentic ways, selecting appropriate technology resources, and collaborating with the learning community to plan, design, implement, and continually refine an effective, student-centered technology plan.

> **Guiding Principle:** School library media specialists use technology from the perspective of a technologist, integrating people, learning, and the tools of technology. They play a critical role in designing student experiences that use the full range of technologies to promote learning, modeling effective uses of technology, and evaluating and selecting appropriate technologies for teaching and learning.

Supporting the Use of Technology across the Curriculum

There is strong consensus in the research community that technology can enhance student learning, but often teachers don't understand information technology broadly enough to apply it to their work with students. Many teachers have not received any kind of technology training and only a small percentage of America's teachers feel comfortable integrating technology into their lessons. As one of the school's experts in information technology, school library media specialists can guide and assist teachers in the use of technology for learning and teaching.

Demonstrating the Tangible Benefits of Using Technology

How can teachers use technology across the curriculum if they don't know what is possible? Teachers need to see tangible and feasible benefits for integrating technology use into teaching and learning. Providing opportunities for teachers to observe best practices is the first step in helping them become comfortable using technology and integrating it into their lesson plans. Because of their expertise in technology processes and products, school library media specialists are especially well positioned to show teachers how technology can be integrated into the curriculum.

School library media specialists can use websites, such as the following, to give teachers a look at what other educators are doing to integrate technology into their teaching.

American Memories Fellows Program. Since 1997 the Library of Congress's National Digital

74

Library has sponsored the American Memory Fellows Program to help schools make powerful educational use of the library's American Memory Collections. Teams of middle and high school humanities teachers and library media specialists from across the country meet each summer to learn how to use the library's unique primary resources and to create exemplary teaching units that are then shared with other educators. Show teachers the units created by the American Memories fellows to demonstrate how technology can be used to enhance learning in the content areas (http://www.edc.org/CCT/NDL/index.html).

Active Learning Sites CyberTour. Take teachers on a virtual tour of the Web to visit sites where students collaborate, locate primary resources, publish their work and experience the Web as an active learning environment (http://www.infosearcher.com/cybertours/index.html).

ICPrize Winners: AASL has a web page highlighting the winners of ICONnect's ICPrize. The ICPrize is awarded to school library media specialist-teacher teams who develop curricular units that demonstrate integration, innovation, curriculum, collaboration, and connection. Discuss the prize-winning projects with teachers to illustrate how technology can support authentic student learning (http://www.ala.org/ICONN/2000icprize.html).

Virtual Architecture: Designing and Directing Curriculum-Based Telecomputing. Share these outstanding curriculum-based educational telecomputing projects with teachers. Teachers will see projects that require students to communicate electronically with other individuals or groups, collect and analyze information, and solve complex information problems (http://ccwf.cc.utexas.edu/~jbharris/VirtualArchitecture/).

WebQuests. A webquest is an outstanding means of combining a teacher's subject area knowledge and a media specialist's research expertise to create a meaningful collaborative project that requires critical thinking and active learning on the part of students. Show teachers the sample webquests located on this website to illustrate how technology can support interdisciplinary teaching and learning (http://edweb.sdsu.edu/webquest/webquest.html).

School library media specialists can also introduce teachers to electronic discussion lists (listservs), discussion groups, and other online environments in which they can communicate with other educators. Teachers need safe supportive environments to ask questions, share ideas, or just chat with other educators about how to integrate technology into their instruction. There are many electronic discussion groups for educators (see Miller, 2000). TAPPED IN™ is a particularly useful electronic workplace for educators. A multiuser virtual environment (MUVE), TAPPED IN™ enables educators from around the world to plan and conduct projects, participate in topical discussions, conduct and attend courses, find resources, experts, and new colleagues, and serve as resources for other educators.

Perhaps most importantly, school library media specialists can model effective technology integration for teachers. Teachers are often hesitant to try something new unless they have seen someone in their school be successful. It is always easier to believe "your" kids can benefit from technology when you have actually seen "your" kids in action. Library Power veterans suggest that the school library media specialist identify one or two teachers who are interested in updating a current unit to include technology. Collaborate on the planning, teaching, and assessment of that unit. Invite other teachers to observe students at work. Then, share the results of the unit with teachers, parents, and community members. Make sure to spend time at a faculty meeting reflecting on how the integration of technology affected student learning.

Teaching Teachers about Technology

Once teachers, and administrators, develop a new understanding of how technological processes and resources can enhance student learning, they must learn how to use technology. School librarians are natural technology leaders. Why? Doug Johnson (2000) provides the following nine reasons why school library media specialists make good technology leaders:

1. School library media specialists have a healthy attitude toward technology. The first question school library media specialists ask is, "How will this technology resource enhance student learning?"

2. School library media specialists are skilled teachers. They understand learning theory

and use effective teaching strategies to guide learning.

3. School library media specialists understand the use of technology in the information literacy process and how it can be used to help foster higher-level thinking skills. For decades, school library media specialists have collaborated with teachers to integrate information literacy skills and technology resources into student projects.

4. School library media specialists are experienced skill integrators and collaborators. Collaboration and integration are the cornerstones of successful school library media programs.

5. School library media specialists serve as models for the successful use of technology. Technology has been a critical part of the school library media program for decades. In fact, as Doug Johnson (2000) points out, in many schools, school library media specialists were the first educators to use technology purposefully.

6. School library media specialists provide in-building support. In Information-Powered schools, school library media specialists have the flexibility and time to model effective technology integration and to act as coaches and mentors.

7. School library media specialists have a whole school view. School library media specialists work with every teacher and student in the building. They have a broad view of the curriculum, student learning needs, teaching styles, resources, and current technology use.

8. School library media specialists are concerned about the ethical use of technology. The library profession has long been a leader in protecting intellectual freedom, copyright, privacy, and the right of all users to receive high-quality library service.

9. School library media specialists can provide the needed leadership in buildings for technology integration. One of the primary jobs of school library media specialists is to stay cur-

rent with educational trends, emerging technologies, new resources (in all formats), and community connections.

Developing the Professional Development Plan

It is unreasonable to expect change from one-hour workshops on how to use an e-mail or conduct an Internet search. Instead, teachers need ongoing opportunities to experiment and explore, to interact with each other, and to experience the benefits of technology integration. The Information Power team should work with the school's technology planning committee to plan, design, and implement effective professional development for teachers —professional development that allows teachers to be part of a community of learners and gives them confidence to integrate technology effectively into the curriculum.

Library Power veterans recommend the following process for creating an effective staff development program in technology:

Step 1: Identify your school's technology "gurus." Form a network of competent technology users in your building to work with the faculty on a continuous basis. On-site technical support is critical when teachers are trying to use technology in their classrooms. If teachers encounter difficulties, they need immediate help and support.

Step 2: Find out about your faculty and staff. Use a formal survey, focus group interviews, or informal discussions in the hallways to ask the faculty about their current level of technology use. Assess their interest in using technology to build problem-solving skills, expand students' learning experiences, communicate with parents, and cooperate with educators.

Step 3: Compile survey responses. Careful analysis of the data and thoughtful conversations about its meaning will result in a comprehensive staff development plan that will help the faculty improve their technology skills and develop technology-rich learning experiences for students.

LIBRARY POWER LESSON

Professional development in technology use will not be successful unless the principal is supportive. It is critical for principals to participate in the technology training so they will have firsthand knowledge of how technology can be used and what problems the staff experiences.

Step 4: Design the staff development program. Make sure the program addresses the needs identified by the faculty in your building. Effective professional development should expose teachers, staff, and administrators to actual practice rather than descriptions of practice, focus on concrete and authentic applications, connect to student learning, and provide opportunities for ongoing observation. Remember: just like students, educators also have different learning styles. No single staff development method will work for everyone. Plan an array of professional development experiences such as mentoring, modeling, ongoing workshops, special courses, structured observations, and summer institutes. See Chapter 3 for information on professional development.

Step 5: Link to other staff development initiatives. Integrating technology into other initiatives within the school and district adds value. In particular, build partnerships with other school-based initiatives that focus on helping students research and solve problems. See Chapter 11 for additional information on creating professional development partnerships.

Step 6: Model effective technology integration. If the goal is for teachers to incorporate the strengths of technology into their instruction, rather than merely adding technology to the way they always have done things, teachers need to observe others successfully integrating technology into their lessons.

Step 7: Provide ongoing support. Support groups, peer coaching, and study groups create avenues for teachers, staff, and principals to tell stories about what worked, what didn't work, and what seemed to make a difference. They give the faculty and staff a place to think about questions such as, "What does technology mean for my classroom?" and "How will technology integration improve learning?"

Step 8: Evaluate the effectiveness of professional development on a regular basis to ensure it is meeting participants' needs. Use evaluation results to improve the content and form of the professional development offered currently and to provide data for future planning. A well-planned, ongoing professional development program is essential if teachers are expected to use technology to empower student learning. School library media specialists must use their expertise in information technology processes to lead the school's professional development efforts to enable and encourage teachers to become "tech-savvy."

> ## LIBRARY POWER LESSON
>
> Truly integrating technology into teaching and learning is a slow, time-consuming process that requires long-term commitment on the part of administrators, teachers, parents, and the community. Without the buy-in of all the stakeholders, the effort will not be successful.

Designing Authentic Learning Experiences

School library media specialists and teachers must work collaboratively to use information technology to create powerful learning experiences for students. Such experiences allow students to work on authentic, meaningful, and challenging problems; to develop information literacy skills and computer competencies; to interact with professionals and members of the broader community; and to understand information technology broadly enough to apply it to their everyday lives.

What Do Authentic Learning Experiences Look Like?

What do authentic learning experiences look like? Authentic learning experiences challenge students to address the types of problems they might encounter in the real world. Students construct their own meanings from their work and produce products and performances that have meaning beyond success in school.

Authentic learning experiences are defined by the following characteristics:

- Disciplined inquiry
- Knowledge construction
- Value beyond school
- Connections to student's personal world
- Cooperation and communication

In authentic learning experiences, just like in real life, technology serves as a tool, helping students solve problems. Technology is used to gather, organize, analyze, and present information. Students can use electronic resources such as encyclopedias and full-text magazine indexes or digitized resources such as the Library of Congress American Memories Collection to gather information. They can communicate with other students from around the world or reach out to scientists, researchers, and other experts using e-mail. Portable technologies, such as laptop computers, can be used to gather data outside the classroom. Tools such as spreadsheets, databases, and graphing software can help students analyze their data. Finally, students can use multimedia-authoring tools such as Power Point, Hyper Studio, or Microsoft FrontPage to present their findings. Technology can also be used to simulate real-life experiences for students. It is not always possible to take the class on an archeological dig or a trip to the rainforest.

Here are several examples of authentic learning experiences that integrate content knowledge with information literacy skills, technology competencies, and communication skills:

Project for third-grade students: You are now being hired as a rainforest animal expert. There are many people who want to get rid of the beautiful rainforest to make money from the land. More than half of all plant and animal species live in the rainforest. Save the Rainforest Project needs your help to tell these companies about so many of these wonderful creatures and why the rainforest is important to these animals. Your job over the next month will be to research and develop a written report, visual project, and be prepared for an oral presentation about an animal that lives in the rainforest. You will need to explain why your animal needs the rainforest to survive. (From Maureen Mooney. *Animals of the Rainforest: A WebQuest for Third Grade.* http://www.mmooney49.1hwy.com/rain.html)

Project for middle school social studies students: The Sell-2-U Advertising Agency is hiring a new advertising team. You and your partner have decided to apply for the job. The company president has asked that all prospective employees analyze some current advertisements to demonstrate their knowledge of advertising techniques. He has also requested that each team create an ad for a fictional product. The team that presents the best ad will get the job. (From Cynthia Matzat. *And*

Now a Word from Our Sponsor: A WebQuest on Propaganda. http://www.thematzats.com/propaganda/)

Project for high school biology students: Design an information system to track HIV testing and notification; communicate the design to potential participants; and convince users that privacy will be maintained. (From AAUW. *Tech-Savvy: Educating Girls in the New Computer Age.* 2000)

How Do the Information Literacy Standards for Student Learning Support Authentic Learning?

Information Power: Building Partnerships for Learning describes the information literacy standards for student learning as "a comprehensive framework for designing and implementing the information-based activities that are the core of authentic learning" (AASL and AECT, 1998, p. 70). The standards broaden the definition of computer literacy beyond a static list of basic computer skills, such as learning to use e-mail or creating a database. Instead, the standards focus on helping students learn to locate, organize, evaluate, and use information to solve complex information problems, address personal goals, and promote lifelong learning.

The first three standards define information-literate students and should be incorporated into all information technology-based activities. Students who are information literate:

Standard 1: Access information efficiently and effectively. Information-literate students recognize the need for information, know when to seek information, how to frame questions, and where to look for information. They know how to structure a search across a variety of sources and formats, and recognize that accurate and comprehensive information is needed to make intelligent decisions.

Standard 2: Evaluate information critically and competently. Information-literate students weigh information carefully, understanding the need to assess its accuracy, validity, relevance, completeness, and impartiality.

Standard 3: Use information accurately and creatively. Information-literate students understand the need to use information to draw conclusions and develop new understandings. They organize and integrate information from a range of sources in order to apply it to decision making, problem solving, critical thinking, and creative expression.

The last three standards address the ethical issues of technology use. As Doug Johnson points out, "applied ethics needs to be an integral part of technology use in schools" (1998). Students need to consider how technology will impact the society and culture in which they live. They need to understand the concepts of privacy, intellectual property, intellectual freedom, and appropriateness. Students who are ethically responsible:

Standard 7: Recognize the importance of information to a democratic society and seek out information from diverse sources, contexts, disciplines, and cultures. They respect and support actively the principle of equitable access to information.

Standard 8: Practice ethical behavior in regard to information and information technology. They apply principles and practices that reflect high ethical standards for accessing, evaluating, and using information. They respect the principles of intellectual freedom, comply with intellectual property rights, and use information technology responsibly.

Standard 9: Participate effectively in groups to pursue and generate information. Students acknowledge and seek the insights and contributions of a variety of cultures and disciplines. They collaborate with diverse individuals to identify information problems, seek their solutions, and communicate these solutions accurately and creatively.

What Steps Are Involved in Creating a Technology-Based Authentic Learning Experience?

Library Power veterans suggest that school library media specialists use the following strategies to create technology-based authentic learning experiences:

Work with students to identify meaningful projects within your school's curriculum frameworks. Help students focus on large concepts and principles. Guide them in choosing a performance task that demonstrates what they have learned and involves a meaningful context, clear purpose, and audience.

Encourage and accept student autonomy and initiative. Allow students to "be in charge" of their learning. Teachers and school library media specialists should act as facilitators and guides, conferencing with students and providing opportunities for them to reflect on their learning throughout the project.

Have students work with primary resources, raw data, physical materials, and people—the types of resources that lawyers, engineers, scientists, scholars, and other professionals use in the real world to tackle problems.

Connect students to resources in the larger community—public and university libraries; government and other public agencies; museums; scientists, researchers, and other experts; and other individuals or agencies interested in solving similar programs.

Have students use technology for data collection, information management, problem solving, decision making, communications, and presentations.

Require students to consider the social and ethical issues related to their problem.

Involve students in the assessment process.

LIBRARY POWER LESSON

Often educators are hesitant to use technology because they are afraid of looking incompetent in front of their students. Use the students' knowledge of technology to your advantage. Invite them to demonstrate how to use new applications, locate appropriate electronic resources, and coach other students.

The WebQuest website provides a template for developing authentic learning experiences that rely on Internet resources. School library media specialists will find webquests especially useful for teachers who are novice technology users. Webquests allow teachers, and school library media specialists, to make an easy transition into developing authentic learning experiences that use technology.

Understanding by Design, by Grant Wiggins and Jay McTighe (ASCD, 1998), provides practical design tools for developing authentic learning activities, including criteria for selecting "big ideas" worthy of study, strategies for framing student learning around essential questions, and a continuum of assessment methods for determining the degree to which students understand. Although

Wiggins and McTighe do not directly address technology use, they do help teachers understand how to design authentic learning experiences.

Selecting Appropriate Technology Resources

A primary reason some teachers are hesitant to integrate technology into their teaching is the difficulty they face finding appropriate technology resources. School library media specialists must guide and assist them in evaluating and selecting appropriate informational and instructional resources. While the topic of technology resource selection is beyond the scope of this chapter, Library Power veterans offer the following advice for school library media specialists:

- Work collaboratively with the school technology coordinator, teachers, students, and parents to select resources.

- Remember: student learning must drive selection. You are wasting time and money if the resource does not connect to the curriculum and motivate students to be active learners.

- Teach teachers and students how to evaluate websites. See ICONnect for Web evaluation tools and resources (http://www.ala.org/ICONN/evaluate.html).

- Develop curriculum resource guides to support specific units of study. See the Nueva Library Page for sample curriculum resource guides (http://nuevaschool.org/~debbie/library/overview.html).

- Consider the needs of students with disabilities. See *Adaptive Technology for the Internet: Making Electronic Resources Accessible to All* (Mates, 2000) for advice on technologies as such as screen readers, Braille screens, voice recognition systems, hearing assistance devices, and HTML coding for accessibility. Use the program Bobby, developed by the Center for Applied Special Technology, to analyze your school and library web page for their accessibility to students with disabilities (http://www.cast.org/bobby/).

- Look for electronic resources that respect the diversity of your student body, staff, and the world. Evaluate websites and other electronic resources for ethnic, racial, cultural, and gender biases.

- Do not be fooled by the glitz of some websites and electronic resources. Flashing graphics, dancing icons, and sound do not necessarily equate with quality.

- Draw on community resources. Provide links to local, state, and regional resources.

- Build and maintain your knowledge of technology resources.

Developing a Student-Centered Technology Plan

To realize the benefits of technology, schools must develop a plan for integrating technology into the curriculum. An effective technology plan focuses on helping students and others become independent, lifelong learners who use information and information technology responsibly and ethically. It ensures that technology strengthens the existing curriculum and supports meaningful, engaged learning for all students. It also addresses how technology use will be supported.

A planning team should be responsible for the development of an overall technology plan. The team should develop a vision for the plan, determine the goals that must be met, and create steps to implement those goals. The focus should be on developing a plan that is based on what students, staff, and administration should be able to do with technology. Expected outcomes should determine the types and amount of technology needed.

How do schools develop effective technology plans and what should be included? The following guidelines are based on the experiences of schools that have successfully integrated technology:

Step 1: Convene a technology planning committee. The planning committee should include the school library media specialist, technology coordinator, administrators, teachers, parents, and community members. District office representatives, potential business partners, a representative from the state department of education and/or a local institution of higher education may also be consulted.

Step 2: Review existing school plans, including the school improvement plan. The school technology plan must support the district's educational mission and goals and reflect existing or anticipated districtwide technology planning. Technology plans are short-lived and rarely implemented if they are not an integral part of the school's overall school improvement plan.

Step 3: Gather information about how students learn, what skills students will need to succeed in the workplace, and how technology can be used to improve education. Become familiar with research on the most promising ways of using technology, available technology, and professional development opportunities and requirements.

Step 4: Generate a collective vision for technology use in your school. The vision should support meaningful, engaged learning for all students, promote technology use for authentic purposes, and encourage integration of the information literacy standards for student learning with subject matter content across the disciplines.

Step 5: Conduct an in-depth analysis of your school's technology needs. Base the assessment on curricular goals and program needs. Describe how the use of technology will align with and expand curricular and instructional objectives. List schoolwide objectives and related activities that describe how technology use supports instruction, enhances the curriculum, and strengthens the school program. The objectives should be directly related to learner and teacher needs.

Step 6: Develop a staff development plan that describes how teachers will become effective users of technology. The focus should be on helping teachers become proficient with technology and providing opportunities for teachers to explore ways to use technology effectively with students.

Step 7: Identify available technology resources in the school and district. Gather data on the information infrastructure, including backbone wiring, networks, distribution systems, telecommunications; locations of technologies; hardware configurations for computers, video, CD-ROM, etc.; software and information packages/data sources; and the repair and maintenance of the information infrastructure. Make sure to identify personnel responsible for the information infrastructure.

Step 8: Develop a budget and funding strategy. The technology plan should provide a budget that includes sufficient funding for each component of the plan. It is critical that money be allocated to provide professional development for teachers. If local school funds are inadequate, develop a plan for seeking money from outside funders such as foundations, government agencies, and local businesses. See Chapter 11 for information on resourcing.

Step 9: Prepare an evaluation plan. The technology plan should provide a general description of the process for evaluating and revising the plan. The evaluation should focus on assessing the effects of technology on teaching and instructional practices and student outcomes. It should provide information that can be used to demonstrate progress, to make revisions to the plan, and to justify funding requests.

Step 10: Write the plan. Chapter headings might include: Vision, Mission Statement and Learning Goals, Implementation Benchmarks and Timelines, Staff Development Strategy, Network and Telecommunications Planning, Long-Term Funding Strategy, and Assessment and Evaluation.

Step 11: Implement, monitor, and revise the plan. Monitoring the implementation process and actively solving problems that arise are essential. Technology planning is an ongoing process. As technology changes, as curriculum and instruction priorities are revised, and as the school grows, the plan must change.

Developing a technology plan is a complex process. The guidelines included here are meant to give you an overview of the process and to emphasize the importance of developing a technology plan that focuses on improving student learning. Consult the resources listed at the end of this chapter for more detailed directions for developing your school's technology plan, including guiding questions for technology planning, planning tables to identify essential tasks and responsibilities, and examples of exemplary school technology plans.

Summing Up

Whether technology should be used in schools is no longer a question. Instead, the current focus is on how technology can be used effectively to enhance student learning. The role of the school library media specialist is clear: help teachers use technology in innovative ways across the curriculum, design student experiences that use technology in authentic ways, select appropriate technology resources, and collaborate with the learning community to plan, design, implement, and continually refine an effective, student-centered technology plan.

Featured Resources for Further Information

Berger, Pam. 1998. *Internet for Active Learners: Curriculum-Based Strategies for K–12.* Chicago: ALA.

Johnson, Doug. 1998. Developing an ethical compass for worlds of learning. *Multimedia Schools* 5 (Nov./Dec.): 42–47.

Loertscher, David V. 1999. *Reinvent Your School's Library in the Age of Technology: A Guide for Principals and Superintendents.* San Jose, Calif.: Hi Willow Research and Publishing.

Mates, Barbara T. 2000. *Adaptive Technology for the Internet: Making Electronic Resources Accessible to All.* Chicago: ALA.

Miller, Elizabeth B. 2000. *The Internet Resource Directory for K–12 Educators and Librarians.* Englewood, Colo.: Libraries Unlimited.

Wiggins, Grant, and Jay McTighe. 1998. *Understanding by Design.* Alexandria, Va.: Association for Supervision and Curriculum Development.

Web Resources

American Association of School Librarians. 2000. *ICONnect: Connecting Learners to Information.* http://www.ala.org/ICONN/

Harris, Judi. 1999. *Virtual Architecture's Web Home.* http://ccwf.cc.utexas.edu/~jbharris/Virtual-Architecture/

Johnson, Doug. June 8, 2000. *The Why, What, How and WHO of Staff Development in Technology: The Growing Importance of Teacher-Librarian's Role in Helping Create Technology-Savvy Educators.* http://www.doug-johnson.com/dougwri/ISISjohnson.htm

McKenzie, J. 2000. *Technology Planning.* http://fno.org/fnoindex.html#Technology

North Central Regional Educational Laboratory. October 12, 2000. *Pathways to School Improvement.* http://www.ncrel.org/sdrs/

8 Flexible Access: Essential to Active Learning

Sandra Hughes-Hassell and Anne Wheelock

Imagine a school library media center where 36 classes file in once each week to search the online catalog, learn about Mr. Dewey's invention, and browse the encyclopedia looking for places and names that have little to do with their classroom curriculum. Now imagine the same school library media center full of students and teachers, all working with the school library media specialist to explore, discover, and share information that expands the scope of their textbooks, a library media program that supports student learning by providing resources and instruction that enables students to actively participate in the learning process. That is the change *Information Power: Building Partnerships for Learning* can bring.

The success of *Information Power: Building Partnerships for Learning* rests on flexible access—access that removes restrictions on when the school library media center can be used and gives students and teachers access to information, ideas, and resources for learning throughout the day. Flexible access makes the other aspects of *Information Power: Building Partnerships for Learning* possible. Perhaps most importantly, flexible access means teachers can work collaboratively with the school library media specialist to provide students with more complex and authentic assignments requiring information literacy skills, and be confident that students will receive the instruction and assistance they need to develop an in-depth understanding of the topic under study.

Guiding Principle: Flexible access is not an end in itself, but a key prerequisite to resource-based teaching and overall implementation of *Information Power: Building Partnerships for Learning*. Flexible access sets the stage for students and teachers to use school library media resources and services at any time during the day or week: to browse, exchange books, read, use electronic resources, or conduct research. And flexible access makes it possible for school library media specialists and teachers to work together to plan, teach, and assess collaboratively developed units.

What Is Flexible Access?

Flexible access has two components—flexible scheduling and open access. Both ensure that the school library media program's resources and services are readily available so that information problems can be solved when they arise.

Flexible Scheduling

Flexible scheduling refers to a flexible and creative schedule that allows students to use the school library media center according to their learning needs, rather than according to a predetermined timetable for weekly or biweekly school library media center classes. In libraries with flexible schedules, teachers and school library media specialists teach together so that students can complete assignments that call on library media resources for learning, *not* because the schedule indicates it is "library time." Flexible scheduling reinforces the collaborative work school library media specialists and teachers do to plan authentic learning activities for students.

Flexible scheduling does not mean simply eliminating the established schedule and "letting it happen." Instead, it means that school library media specialists and teachers work together to develop a schedule that makes the school library media program's resources and services available for all, regardless of ability, at any time. The schedule is dynamic and changes constantly as learning goals change. It permits whole classes as well as small groups and individuals to use the school library media center spontaneously—when the need arises or when certain aspects of a subject pique student curiosity.

Open Access

Open access ensures that despite the elimination of the weekly library period, students continue to use the school library media center on a regular basis to exchange books, receive guidance in selecting appropriate reading materials, read, and tap into all the school library media center's information resources. Open access does not mean there is no plan for circulation of library media materials. To the contrary, open access requires a coherent plan for the circulation of materials. It requires careful and systematic thinking about how the library media center schedule can ensure that all students will use the center on a regular basis to browse and select materials for their assignments and pleasure reading at least once a week. Open access also means offering services beyond the school day, including extended hours, interlibrary loan services, parent and community programs, and after-hours remote access.

Characteristics of Flexible Scheduling and Open Access

Students' and teachers' needs determine how and when the school library media center is used.

The school library media center accommodates students of different age levels and grades simultaneously.

The school library media center is used all day by students involved in a variety of independent and group activities.

The school library media center is available for classes, small groups, and individuals.

Information literacy standards for student learning are taught within the context of the classroom curriculum.

Students learn to locate and use resources through frequent practice.

Teachers and the school library media specialist schedule instruction for blocks of time.

Teachers view the school library media center as an extension of their classrooms and the school library media program as central to student learning.

Students, teachers, and parents have unrestricted opportunities to use electronic and print resources, audiovisual materials, and other media within and beyond the school day.

> **LIBRARY POWER LESSON**
>
> *Recruit parents to keep the library media center open after-hours and on Saturdays.* At one school in Raleigh, North Carolina, the school library media specialist taught fathers how to circulate media center resources and provide reader assistance. Thanks to the dedication of these fathers, the school library media center is now open on Saturday mornings for parents to use with their children.

Planning for Flexible Access

Moving from a predetermined schedule for school library media center use to a more flexible schedule challenges a variety of school routines and beliefs about student learning. This is a change that asks teachers to think through the views they hold about students as lifelong learners, about the skills they need for future learning, and about how their own teaching integrates with school library media center resources. For some teachers, the thought of students in the early grades traveling to the school library media center on their own challenges stereotypes of which students they can trust with what responsibilities. Other teachers may worry that precious and scarce school library media resources will disappear without strict supervision of their checkout and use.

What can you do to set the stage for this change? Making flexible access part of your school's regular routine involves:

- Learning about flexible access
- Planning for scheduling changes
- Developing an implementation timetable

Learning about Flexible Access

The Information Power team is responsible for guiding the school community toward flexible access. This means the team must be clear about how flexible scheduling and open access work and why they best serve the needs of students, teachers, staff, and parents (see Table 8.1). As a first step, you should collect materials on flexible access for your Information Power team to read and discuss.

As a second step, the Information Power team should visit schools where school library media specialists have implemented flexible access with positive results. See Chapter 3 for advice on how to get the most out of your visit. During your visit:

- Observe the school library media program in action.
- Watch students use and circulate resources independently.
- Ask the school library media specialist, teachers, principal, and students questions about the move to flexible access.

If your team cannot visit a school, telephone or e-mail the school library media specialist with your questions and concerns and seek out videos the team can view and discuss. Use Information Power team meetings and faculty meetings to discuss flexible access and to begin to identify ways it might work in your school.

Planning for Scheduling Changes

Once your Information Power team understands the value and importance of flexible access, it is time to begin a more detailed planning process. This involves rearranging the school library media center to allow simultaneous use by all grade levels and devel-

TABLE 8.1
Benefits of Flexible Access

Benefits of Flexible Access
• Teachers can take advantage of the spontaneity of the teachable moment and send students to the school library media center when interest is high.
• Teachers can collaborate with the school library media specialist for team teaching and collaboratively developed units.
• Teachers can work with the school library media specialist to integrate the *Information Literacy Standards for Student Learning* into the curriculum of the classroom.
• Students learn research and information literacy skills they will use as lifelong learners.
• Students become independent users of resources.
• Students interact with other students and teachers from different classes and grade levels.
• Students develop a sense of responsibility for their own learning.

From Flexible Access Library Media Programs by Jan Buchanan. 1991. Libraries Unlimited. (800-237-6124) or www.lu.com.

oping new schedules so teachers can sign up to use the school library media center for both small group and whole class instruction.

REARRANGING THE SCHOOL LIBRARY MEDIA CENTER

The layout of the school library media center can either encourage or impede flexible access. Physical arrangements of furniture and space must allow large groups, small groups, and individuals to use the school library media center simultaneously. The traffic pattern should allow children freedom of movement to all areas of the center without disrupting ongoing activities.

SETTING UP A SCHEDULE

The school library media center sign-up schedule you adopt reflects the way your team expects students and teachers to use the school library media center. The schedule should make it clear that you look forward to multiple activities taking place in the center simultaneously. Some centers are large enough to accommodate three or four scheduled activities as well as use by individual students. Even the smallest school library media center space can allow for independent circulation of books by individual students and scheduled or spontaneous use by small groups or individuals.

When the Information Power team is designing the school library media center schedule, make sure the new schedule:

- Accommodates individual students throughout the day
- Includes time for classes and/or small group visits
- Indicates time for collaborative planning and meetings;
- Varies the school library media specialist's lunch and administrative time each day
- Includes opportunities for students and parents to visit the school library media center before school and after school

Different schools develop different schedules to reflect distinct approaches to teaching and learning. The following example from the Philadelphia Library Power Project demonstrates one approach to flexible access. Other examples can be found in *Flexible Access Library Media Programs* (Buchanan, 1991) and *Power Up Your Library* (Salmon et al., 1996).

FLEXIBLE ACCESS AT HARRINGTON ELEMENTARY SCHOOL

Harrington Elementary School has approximately 700 students in grades K–4. There are four classes on each grade level. The school library media center is staffed with one professional school library media specialist. Student volunteers work in the school library media center on a daily basis.

The school library media specialist and classroom teachers work closely together to plan curriculum-related activities. Formal planning takes place at weekly small learning community meetings. The school library media specialist usually attends one small learning community meeting per week. She also plans with individual teachers, or small groups of teachers, formally and informally several times each week.

Children in grades 1–4 visit the school library media center in small groups for book exchange before and during the school day. They may also visit with their class or as members of small groups. A child in a third grade class, for example, might come to the school library media center several times in one week: four times with a small group to borrow books, three times with her class to conduct research, and two times in a small group to create a multimedia presentation.

The kindergarten classes at Harrington are located across the street in an annex. Children in kindergarten visit the school library media center with their class once per week for book exchange and to hear a story. Classroom teachers supervise the book exchanges and conduct the story hours. Kindergarten children may also come to the school library media center at other times. For example, a child in kindergarten might come with a small group to research mammals with the school library media specialist, or the teaching assistant might bring him for independent book exchange.

Even when the school library media specialist is working with a whole class or a small group of students, the school library media center is open for small groups of students to exchange books, work on research, use the computers, or read. Students handle circulation of their own materials. Student volunteers recard materials and reshelve resources.

The school library media specialist posts the school library media center schedule on Friday mornings. Each half hour block of time is divided into two sections indicating that two scheduled activities may take place each half hour. Before the schedule is posted, the school library media specialist reserves time for her scheduled work with students, collaborative planning with teachers, administrative work, and lunch (see Figure 8.1).

PROVIDING ACCESS TO THE SCHEDULE

To encourage new scheduling practices, post the library media schedule in a place that allows all teachers access to it. For example, you might:

Keep the schedule in your own planning book and leave it open on the circulation desk or your office desk.

Put the schedule on large chart paper, laminate the paper, and post it on an easel near the entrance to the school library media center so that anyone can see at a glance the types of activities taking place. Teachers use washable markers to sign up for times they want to use the school library media center. Posting the schedule on a chart also gives teachers more flexibility and independence, and those who feel awkward about writing in the school library media specialist's plan book will feel more comfortable writing on the chart.

Adapt wall calendars into large-format schedules.

Use a software calendaring tool to schedule school library media center visits. Give teachers access to the calendar through the school's local area network.

Assure teachers that they may sign up any time to use the school library media center. For example, if Mr. DiCicco's students become interested in learning about frogs after a student brings one to school on Monday, make sure Mr. DiCicco knows that he may sign up to bring his class to the school library media center to do research on frogs on Tuesday, or even Monday afternoon if space is available.

ESTABLISHING PROCEDURES

In the absence of a guaranteed weekly visit to the school library media center for book checkout, schools that reschedule their library programs more flexibly need to develop new routines to ensure that all students will continue to have access and can move freely between classrooms and the school library media center. Planning for student access to a flexibly scheduled school library media center requires thinking through a plan for independent checkout of materials that addresses these questions: How will teachers monitor student use of the school library media center? How will students and teachers check out school library media center resources? In the process of adopting an independent checkout system, be sure to address the concerns some teachers have about accounting for their students and their use of time. Remember, you can foster independent learning and encourage students' spontaneous use of the school library media center and also adopt a formalized system for circulation. These are not mutually exclusive.

Formalized circulation systems may be as simple as creating school library media center passes using readily accessible materials. For example, depending on the size of your school and the school library media center, you might give each classroom two, three, four, or five passes. Plastic shelf markers (available from library supply vendors), paint sticks, and laminated circulation cards or index cards make good hall passes.

When teachers prefer a system that is less hit-and-miss, consider designing a record-keeping system to help keep track of student visits to the library media center. For example, a fifth-grade teacher might divide his class into five library media center groups. On Monday, Group 1 goes to the library media center, on Tuesday, Group 2, and so on. A first-grade teacher might include the library media center as a learning center or literacy center. Each day she might assign four or five students to the library media center during language arts. The children might browse, exchange books, read, write, use computers, or listen to stories at a listening center.

LIBRARY POWER LESSON

Keep a regular count of the number of students using the school library media center. A month-by-month count of center users will help you follow trends in library media center use and provide data you can use in reporting to your school board and other community partners, planning for future program changes, and developing requests for additional funding and resources.

DEVELOPING AN INDEPENDENT CHECKOUT SYSTEM

Independent checkout is a key aspect of flexible access. It is also something that many school library

FIGURE 8.1

Harrington Elementary School Schedule for Week of April 15

	Monday	Tuesday	Wednesday	Thursday	Friday
9:00-9:30	Book checkout	Book checkout Anderson—small group research	Book checkout Meet with Anderson (gr. 1) to develop rubric	Book checkout Library Power librarian's meeting (9:00-12:00)	Book checkout
9:30-10:00	Whole class K—book checkout Anderson—small group research	Math tutors Anderson—small group research	Library administration	Library Power librarian's meeting (9:00-12:00) Math tutors	Whole class K—book checkout
10:00-10:30	Anderson—small group research Whole class K—book checkout	Anderson—small group research Math tutors	Meet with environment small learning community	Library Power librarian's meeting (9:00-12:00) Math tutors	
10:30-11:00	Anderson—small group research 100 book challenge, Gr. 2	Anderson—small group research Math tutors	100 book challenge, Gr. 2	Library Power librarian's meeting (9:00-12:00) Math tutors	
11:00-11:30	Anderson—small group research	Library Administration 100 book challenge, Gr. 4	Whole Class K—book checkout	Library Power librarian's meeting (9:00-12:00) 100 book challenge, Gr. 4	Library administration 100 book challenge, Gr. 4
11:30-12:00	Librarian's lunch	Whole class K—book checkout Meet with Curry (Gr. 4) to discuss under-the-sea unit		Library Power librarian's meeting (9:00-12:00)	Librarian's lunch
12:00-12:30	Literature discussion group—Andy (Gr. 4)	Librarian's lunch	Literature discussion group—Andy (Gr. 4)	Librarian's lunch	Literature discussion group—Andy (Gr. 4)
12:30-1:00		Literature discussion group—Andy (Gr. 4)	Librarian's lunch	Literature discussion group—Andy (Gr. 4)	
1:00-1:30	Meet with Hirshfeld (Gr. 1) to discuss animal unit	Anders (Gr. 2)— work on Kid Pix® slide show on plants	Anders (Gr. 2)— work on Kid Pix® slide show on plants	Anders (Gr. 2)— work on Kid Pix® slide show on plants	Anders Gr. 2)— work on Kid Pix® slide show on plants
1:30-2:00	Introduce unit on simple machines with Banks (Gr. 3)	Banks—research simple machines (whole class)	Banks—research simple machines (whole class)	Banks—research simple machines (whole class)	
2:00-2:30		Banks—research simple machines (whole class)	Banks—research simple machines (whole class)	Banks—research simple machines (whole class)	
2:30-3:00	Library administration Book checkout	Book checkout	Book checkout	Book checkout	Library administration Book checkout

media specialists and teachers struggle to imagine. Teachers worry that students will not be able to find materials they need and that they will waste time "goofing off" in the library media center. School library media specialists worry that resources will disappear and that students will interrupt instruction to ask for help in checking out materials. Experienced Library Power practitioners use several strategies for addressing these concerns, often selecting one approach over others depending on the staff and resources available. For example:

When staffing allows, school library media specialists may assign the job of materials circulation to a library media assistant. The library assistant is responsible for checking resources in and out, helping students locate materials, and keeping students on task.

When a core of diligent volunteers, willing to come on scheduled days and find a substitute if they cannot do so, is available, school library media specialists may assign the job of materials circulation to these helpers.

In some schools, teachers sign up to bring their whole classes for checkout of materials only. The teachers accompany their students to the school library media center and take responsibility for the noise level, straightening up the center, and assisting students in selection and checkout.

Some schools use student assistants for circulation. With the proper instruction, students can be responsible for circulation and helping students locate resources.

In many schools, circulation of materials is the responsibility of the individual student. School library media specialists develop circulation procedures and routines which they explain carefully to students during library orientation. Even kindergarten children can scan materials in and out with the proper training—sometimes they are more diligent about it than the older students.

Developing an Implementation Timetable

Once you have thought through your plans for scheduling and circulation, your Information Power team must develop an implementation plan. Now is the time to present your proposed schedule and procedures to the school-site management team and whole faculty, revising plans in response to their suggestions and concerns. This is also the time to decide on your timetable for implementation.

Some schools prefer to adopt flexible access schoolwide, involving all students and teachers, beginning at the start of a new school year or semester. Other schools may prefer to phase in new scheduling routines. Sometimes teachers of older children are more willing to try flexible scheduling than those of younger children.

Schools may also decide to implement a transition period, during which the school library media center offers both fixed weekly checkout periods and more opportunities for students to visit the school library media center in small groups or on their own. One thing is certain: Whatever degree of flexibility you develop, expect more students to use your school library media center more frequently each week than they would when a fixed schedule is in place.

Executing Your Plan

Students, teachers, staff, and parents need support making the shift from fixed scheduling to flexible access. Regardless of the timetable you choose, teachers and administrators will need time to understand the premises that support flexible access and to think through how this practice will affect students. Be prepared for questions. The next section can help your Information Power team anticipate and answer teacher's and administrator's concerns.

Answering the Most Frequently Asked Questions about Flexible Access

For some educators concerned with the responsibilities of managing large numbers of students, imagining exactly how flexible access fits with the variety of daily requirements and contract obligations can be a challenge. What are the most pressing concerns? How do Library Power veterans respond?

When administrators ask:

If we adopt flexible access, we won't be able to count on the school library media specialist to work with whole classes of students during teachers' planning periods and preparation time. What alternatives do we have?

You respond:

Schools can make alternative arrangements for teacher preparation times. Begin by raising your concerns with the Information Power team or leadership team at your school. Creative solutions to problems can often be worked out by a group. In one Library Power school, the music teacher and science teacher (both members of the Library Power Team) volunteered to cover the six prep times per week normally covered by the school library media specialist. Three days per week they worked as a team to provide instruction for two combined classes. Other options to explore include:

- Designing a rotation schedule for specialist teachers. For example, each student would receive instruction in physical education three days per week and in art or music one day per week.

- Using Title I funding to hire additional personnel to work with the students during teacher's planning time.

- Employing permanent substitutes to supervise classes during teacher's planning time. Activities that require minimum preparation, but maximum benefit (sustained silent reading in the intermediate grades or reading aloud in the primary grades) can be scheduled for these times.

- Reviewing the school budget to look for other funds that can be reallocated to support another specialist to work with students.

When administrators ask:

If we adopt more flexible scheduling practices, how can I be sure all my teachers will use the school library media center effectively?

You respond:

The principal, school library media specialist, and teachers share responsibility for ensuring that *all* students use the school library media center. The principal must continue to monitor library media center use and make sure teachers and the school library media specialist are developing assignments that involve all students in utilizing information literacy skills. Specifically, principals can:

- Attend monthly grade group meetings. Suggest ways teachers might incorporate school library media center services and resources into instruction.

- Review lesson plans on a monthly basis. Look specifically for ways in which teachers are using the school library media center, and if use is not evident, communicate with teachers and school library media specialists.

- Monitor the weekly library media center schedule. Note which classes are using the school library media center and which seem to be absent and raise concerns with teachers and the school library media specialist.

- Recognize teachers and the school library media specialist for successfully incorporating use of the school library media program into their instruction.

When teachers ask:

How do I make sure all my children visit the school library media center after we stop using a regular weekly schedule?

You respond:

It is no secret that flexible scheduling raises worries that some children will slip through the cracks. But this is not necessarily the result of flexible scheduling! Some teachers require students who need extra help in "the basics" to stick to their class work "for their own good," skipping research until they seem more "ready to handle it." Some teachers are reluctant to trust their more impulsive students with unsupervised time.

Developing a schoolwide system of school library media center passes and procedures for independent checkout helps reassure individual teachers that they alone are not responsible for students, but that the whole school is taking responsibility for new routines. Teachers who worry that some students are not taking advantage of school library media center resources, and those who are fearful that some students are not ready for the library media program, benefit from raising these concerns with the school library media specialist, principal, and other teachers. Remember, becoming an information-literate student is *not* a privilege or reward for only the "advanced" or "well-behaved" students. All students need opportunities to develop information literacy skills, and they need regular access to the school library media center to do so.

When teachers ask:

What happens if everybody comes to the school library media center at once?

You respond:

Flexible access does not mean a free-for-all. The classroom teacher's weekly schedule will continue to regulate use of the school library media center by small groups and classes. And in practice, open access extends only to the number of passes each classroom teacher receives. For example, if each teacher has four passes, in a school with 20 classes, no more than 80 individual students are able to visit the school library media center at one time. This may still sound like an unmanageable number. But it is important to remember that it is unlikely that all 20 teachers will send students during the same time interval.

When teachers ask:

What about unsupervised groups of students moving through the hallways? How do we know they will be quiet and won't waste time? And what about students who have difficulty controlling their behavior?

You respond:

Because one goal of the Information-Powered school is to encourage students to become more responsible, independent school library media center users, implementation of *Information Power: Building Partnerships for Learning* can establish new school norms. In many of the Library Power schools, flexible access was the first sign students had ever had that teachers trusted them to act responsibly; as a result, they redefined themselves as learners. As one student put it: "People know that the teacher trusts us. . . . You don't have to go down as a class. . . . It's better and easier. You can look for your *own* book." Said another, "I can think for myself."

Flexible access challenges teachers to help students develop habits of self-discipline that match new expectations for learning. As teachers communicate these expectations, students adjust to new standards for "the way we do things around here" and are less willing to lose "library time" by acting irresponsibly. But it is up to the adults in the school to take time to teach students directly about these standards.

Set clear expectations for student behavior on the way to and from the school library media center and in the center itself. Students need to know the rules and the consequences for breaking them. Post the rules in the school library media center and in the classrooms. Send a copy of the rules home to parents.

Follow through with consequences. If students know they will lose their pass for one week for disruptive behavior on the way to the school library media center, take the pass away from them. Use the opportunity to discuss with students some alternative ways of behaving should a similar situation arise again. When you return the pass, review expected behavior and review alternatives to some "What if . . ." circumstances with the student.

When teachers ask:

I'm worried about losing books and other resources. How do I make sure my students check out books and don't just leave the school library media center with them?

You respond:

Many teachers, especially those in schools without library media assistants, worry about resources and books disappearing from the school library media center. In practice, however, as student ownership and sense of belonging to the school library media center increases, loss of materials declines. When students borrow resources because they want to, not because the teacher or school library media specialist insists they must, they begin to develop intrinsic motivation to return the materials. They are eager to borrow additional resources and realize that the only way to do so is to return the materials they have borrowed.

Likewise, as students learn new habits, they become diligent about checking materials out, and often coach other students in new procedures. Try this approach developed at one Library Power school: When a small group visits the school library media center for book checkout, appoint one student in the group as the monitor. It is this student's job to make sure each child in the group checks out his book properly.

Introducing New Scheduling Practices to Faculty and Staff

Introducing flexible access to teachers, teaching assistants, and other staff members involves the following:

- Explaining the benefits of flexible scheduling and open access to everyone involved.

- Introducing hall passes and other more formal systems for monitoring student use.

- Teaching everyone how students will check out resources independently.

- Discussing expectations for student behavior.

- Explaining how the scheduling process will work—how and when staff may sign up to use the school library media center.

- Emphasizing that flexible access must be in place in order for the library media program to support student learning.

Introducing Flexible Access to Students

Like faculty and staff, students need guidance and instruction as they become accustomed to new scheduling routines. Certainly you are likely to encounter some hurdles in the first few weeks, even months, of your plan. However, preparing students for new expectations can help you minimize problems. Experienced Library Power practitioners suggest:

- Scheduling library orientation for each class in the school.

- Presenting independent checkout and open access as exciting opportunities for learning.

- Teaching students explicitly how to check out materials independently.

- Making behavior expectations clear.

> **LIBRARY POWER LESSON**
>
> *Principals can work as advocates for flexible scheduling by taking advantage of any opening to encourage teachers to try out the collaborative teaching that flexible scheduling makes possible.* Sometimes just reminding teachers of the new schedule and the expectations that go with it can be the push teachers need to try new approaches.

> **LIBRARY POWER LESSON**
>
> *Take as much time as each class needs to teach students (and teachers) how to find materials and check out books.* Students do not automatically understand what it means to become an independent school library media center user and learner. They need explicit guidance over time. One session is not likely to be enough; expect to repeat your instructions on multiple occasions.

Introducing Flexible Access to Parents

Parent support is critical to the success of flexible access. Parents need to be assured that even though their children no longer have weekly "library class," they do have the opportunity to visit the school library media center to check out materials, do research, and use computers at a minimum of once per week. Parents also need to be informed about their children's responsibilities for returning books.

Ongoing community engagement practices—including recruiting parents as school library media center volunteers—can generally involve parents in all aspects of the library media program. In addition, to maximize parent understanding of flexible scheduling in particular:

- Attend parent association meetings.

- Invite parents to the school library media center for "grand openings," school open house nights, and occasions that provide an opening to describe the library media program for parents.

- Send a letter explaining open access and independent checkout home with students.

Summing Up

Information Power: Building Partnerships for Learning challenges school communities to place learning needs above class schedules, school hours, student categorizations, and other logistical concerns. To meet learning needs, stimulate intellectual curiosity, and promote authentic learning, schools are urged to provide flexible, equitable, and far-reaching access to the library media program and to adopt practices such as flexible scheduling and open access which allow information problems to be solved when they arise.

Featured Resources
for Further Information

Browne, Karen Stevens, and Linda Burton. 1989. Timing is everything: Adapting to the flexible schedule. *School Library Journal* 35(14): 20–23.

Buchanan, Jan. 1991. *Flexible Access Library Media Programs.* Englewood, Colo.: Libraries Unlimited.

Salmon, Shelia, Elizabeth K. Goldfarb, Melinda Greenblatt, Anita Phillips Strauss, and Fund for New York City Public Education. 1996. *Power Up Your Library: Creating the New Elementary School Library Program.* Englewood, Colo.: Libraries Unlimited.

Web Resources

Project Better (Building Effective Teaching through Educational Research). Maryland State Department of Education.
http://www.mdk12.org/practices/good_instruction/projectbetter/index.html

Shannon, Donna M. February, 2000. *Flexible Access Library Media Programs Bibliography.*
http://www.libsci.sc.edu/shannon/flexbib.htm

9 Refurbishing for Learning

Cleveland Education Fund, Cleveland, Ohio

Motivating all students and teachers to improve learning and engage in resource-rich work requires redesigning the architectural layout, light, and color scheme of school library media centers. It means transforming unattractive rooms in old, neglected facilities into bright, inviting spaces that shout, "There's something new and different going on here!" In newer facilities, it means rethinking the way space is used and creating more flexible, learning-centered work areas. In some buildings, refurbishing may even mean turning a cluster of classrooms into multimedia centers, wired for the technology of the twenty-first century. Whatever the need or level of resources, refurbishing ensures that the physical environment specifically meets the learning and information needs of students, teachers, and others.

> **Guiding Principle:** The school library media center's physical layout must complement and enhance *Information Power: Building Partnerships for Learning*'s focus on learning that engages students in using multiple information resources to delve into complex problems.

Physical Renovations for the Information-Powered School Library Media Center

Implementation of *Information Power: Building Partnerships for Learning*'s vision requires a physical space that is inviting, attractive, and conducive to learning. Refurbished school library media centers should provide space for large group instruction; however, space must also accommodate multiple activities—small group projects, students working in pairs, individuals conducting research, and many individuals concurrently circulating resources. There must be computer areas for students and staff, instructional areas, and places where students can simply curl up with a good book.

By infusing new life into old space, the physical transformation of the school library media center challenges "business as usual." A new environment and materials to go with it encourage skeptical teachers to embark on more collaborative practice and engage all students in richer inquiry-based assignments. Involving teachers, parents, and administrators in refurbishing builds momentum for change and expands "ownership" for the school library media program. Community partners who invest in the school library media center's physical space are eager to continue to be a part of the activities that take place there.

Developing a Refurbishing Plan

Planning for refurbishing begins with setting goals, identifying the tasks that need to be done, and figuring out the personnel and materials needed to complete those tasks. Setting the stage for the refurbishing work also involves:

94

- Polling school library media center users about their "dream library media center."
- Developing a design for your refurbished school library media center.
- Drawing up a timeline that identifies tasks to be done at different stages.
- Developing a budget to execute your design.

Refurbishing school library media centers is a complex process. Draw on the help of teachers, your technology coordinator, district administrators, parents, community volunteers, and professional experts to participate in each of these planning tasks. Their involvement from the beginning will establish a strong foundation for their participation in later stages of renovations and in other aspects of *Information Power: Building Partnerships for Learning.*

Polling Teachers and Students about Their Dream Library Media Center

Polling students, teachers, administrators, and parents about their dream library media center will capture the interest of "bystanders," identify school needs, and point you toward a school library media center design that meets those needs. You can also use refurbishing surveys to slip in a question about users' hopes and views of the broader library media program. The more responses obtained, the more ideas you will generate to make your school library media center fit your school. Great ideas for book drops, individual reading areas, comfortable chairs, and "reading-only" couches (requiring a book) will come from your "dream library media center" surveys.

The survey process and its results can go a long way toward developing widespread awareness of

---

LIBRARY POWER LESSON

Refurbishing school library media centers is not a single-person project. Those responsible for refurbishing will need to draw on all their collaborative leadership skills to motivate and coordinate the many teams necessary to do the work effectively. Physical renovations require the cooperation of many individuals, including appropriate school district department directors who can assign personnel to make structural repairs and complete basic wall painting. You will need their assistance, especially if scaffolding or special equipment is needed or if you are making renovations to enhance access to students with disabilities. The district library media supervisor can make contact with buildings and maintenance staff in the central office. You will also need to engage custodial staff at your school. At every stage of the refurbishing process, expect to work closely with community partners to recruit help from experts, professionals, and volunteers from across your community.

---

the goals of the school library media program. To generate the widest possible response to your poll, to increase interest in the library media program and the renovations process, and to make the most of survey findings:

Keep surveys simple. Ask responders to place completed surveys in a colorful, centrally located suggestion box. Consider a grid format and fill in the blank questions to add variety and engage interest. Three simple surveys appear at the end of this chapter.

Use different colors for different target groups for easy identification and compilation of responses for each group.

Be sure to summarize all responses in a brief report to your Information Power team, school-based community (including all teachers, parents, and students), and the broader community through the local press, and at meetings of your school board and community partners.

Developing a Design for Your School Library Media Center

The next step in planning for refurbishing is to develop a design that sends a message of welcome and affirms the notion that reading and learning from many information sources are rich and rewarding. Remember, a design that works is a design that puts students at the center of school library use. As one Cleveland school library media specialist observed, "Our library media center is not a place where students *visit,* it's a place where students *belong.*" Survey suggestions can begin discussions about the shape a new design plan should take. Those recruited for the design committee may gather additional ideas from visits to other school library media centers.

As you develop your plan, the design committee must consider the components of the school library media program described in *Information Power: Building Partnerships for Learning* and determine how the facility's design will support each:

Learning and teaching: curricular needs, faculty and staff instructional needs, collaborative planning and teaching, student recreational reading interests, and community and parent instructional needs.

Information access and delivery: access to technology and print resources, leisure reading areas, study areas, signage and display areas.

Technology: integration of technology into learning and teaching, production areas, presentation areas, computer work areas.

Program administration: circulation, supervision, planning, work areas, and storage, networking.

Connections to the community: community access, technological links to community resources.

Developing an effective design requires assessing the space available for optimum use of the facility. No single overall design works in every school. Some schools have expansive areas that lend themselves to extensive school library media center redesign. Others offer little more than classroom-size space for a school library media center that may seem almost an afterthought. In some schools, new design will involve redesigning open space library media centers built in the 1960s. In others, plans will focus on renovating cavernous basement rooms in century-old buildings. A new floor plan of shelving and furniture can improve any space, no matter how large or small, to support the school library media program. Remember that ease of access is critical to ensuring that all students and community members use the school library media center. Be sure to plan for entrance doors wide enough to accommodate wheel chairs, and plan the library media center location so that all students can manage regular visits.

As you plan your design, consider how you can take maximum advantage of the available space to meet the educational needs and instructional activities of all school library media center users. Think about how you might organize your renovations around a curriculum theme, featuring an ocean, desert, or rainforest habitat, archeological site, or urban neighborhood. Different uses suggest different kinds of memorable design features that set off your center as unique. For example:

A reading loft designed as a tree house may invite several youngsters at a time to stretch out with good books of their choosing.

A seat-cushioned bay window may encourage individual students to work quietly on special assignments.

A well-organized parent corner, stocked with information about job training programs, books that parents themselves select, and current magazines in the language of their home, may boost interest among parents who know they can drop into the school library media center at their convenience.

Determining Who Can Help

A team that includes both design professionals and school library media center users is ideal for leading your effort. As you look for those with design expertise:

Seek out a design and architectural professional with specific experience in public space layout and design to be the point person on this phase of the project. That person may come from your own school district or join you as a volunteer from your community.

Work with design experts to determine the manageability and economical use of materials.

Ask for assistance and donated time of design and color experts from local paint corporations, hardware supply stores, other design-oriented businesses, or local schools of design and architecture.

Then involve a variety of others including:

- The school district's library media division staff
- The school's technology coordinator
- Interested teachers, custodial staff, parents, and students from your school
- A knowledgeable public library employee or volunteer
- Vocational-technical program teachers and students

The American Library Association's publication, *Designing a School Library Media Center for the Future* (Erickson and Markuson, 2001) offers further indispensable information for those embarking on library media center refurbishing.

Selecting Materials for Renovations

As your planning proceeds, begin to consider the materials you will use. While some library media centers require extensive overhaul, you can make a major difference with paint, new window treatments, new furniture, floor covering, and accessories.

PAINT

In warm colors, paint is the best deal for your refurbishing dollar. Freshly painted walls make a dramatic impact in a renovated school library media center. Paint can also accessorize a room and add interesting touches. Consider the following:

Aim for an overall color palette selected from a broad spectrum of warm and inviting colors for use against a backdrop of bright ivory walls or for use in their entirety or in combinations for window and door trims, bulletin board frames, bookshelves, and library fixtures. Renovators should plan for the type of paint that will best match the skills of the painters doing the work and the surfaces that need painting. If professionals or school district tradespeople are doing the painting, an oil-base paint is the best and most durable choice. If volunteers are painting, latex paint suits the painting of walls, window frames, and metal shelves you have "roughed" or lightly sanded—and for easy cleanup as well. If your shelves are chipped and scratched from wear, tear, and heavy use, plan to add a coat of polyurethane.

In old buildings with exposed pipes, steam radiators, or other unsightly features, use various colors to emphasize the art deco structures and create unusual effects and focal points.

Turn a battered old circulation desk into a standout feature by painting its base in a bright color and adorning it with a new laminate top.

Paint the drawers of worn file cabinets in varied or alternating colors to attract curious students to check out the contents of clippings and brochures.

WINDOW TREATMENTS

Window treatments and coverings are almost always needed and wanted in the refurbishing project. Blinds, verticals, or curtains prevent glare and offer the convenience of darkening the room for use of audiovisual equipment. Most school library media specialists are thrilled to replace yellowed and torn window shades. Miniblinds are available at some home improvement stores and can be cut to custom sizes by a salesperson while you wait. Installation is not difficult, but be accurate in measuring to avoid a costly mistake. Plan to customize each school's window treatments by "toppers" or curtains that add a unique touch and coordinate with a particular theme.

FURNITURE

Furniture is the most costly aspect of school library media center refurbishing. Make sure that furniture sizes vary in order to meet the needs and ages of the student population. When you buy new furniture, order bigger, sturdier chairs for middle and high school students. Investigate all avenues and sources to make furniture dollars stretch as far as possible. At certain times of the year, some vendors offer free shipping, which can cut costs of new furniture significantly. You may find a treasure trove of sturdy used wooden furniture in your district's central warehouse. For a special activity area, look for six or eight matching chairs offered at an economical price at a used office furniture store.

ACCESSORIES

Accessories make the environment of any ordinary school library media center special and are magnets that draw in reluctant readers and learners. Visual attractions can range from bean-

---

LIBRARY POWER LESSON

Remember, decorating a school library media center is not the same as decorating a home. Window treatments and other fabrics used in the center need to be fire-retardant. Electrical work must meet existing code standards. Particleboard computer stations and other low-cost furniture will not hold up to the heavy use demands placed on your new space. Spend the extra money needed to meet public and commercial building standards. Be alert to special conditions that can raise costs. Structural changes in the walls, ceiling, and flooring of old schools may expose asbestos. If you find asbestos, plan to increase your budget (adding $3,500 for asbestos removal for a 1,500-square-foot library) and extend the renovation timetable.

bag chairs in striking colors to oven mitts and golf club covers used as hand puppets. Empty plastic containers in primary colors make useful storage boxes for crayons or scratch paper. Stuffed animal reading buddies or an in-progress giant jigsaw puzzle might just catch the attention of a wary student. The ideas for these extras are unlimited.

Planning for New Technology

School library media centers of the twenty-first century will be increasingly "wired" and oriented to new information technologies. As you plan for refurbishing, develop a school technology plan (see Chapter 7). The plan should describe the essential elements of the information infrastructure, including backbone wiring, networks, distribution systems, telecommunications throughout the school and the library media center; locations of technologies; hardware configurations for computers, video, CD-ROM, and so on; repair and maintenance of the

information infrastructure; personnel responsible for the information infrastructure; initial costs versus ongoing costs; and software and information packages/data sources that will be made available and where. A technology plan will save you money, time, and frustration in the long run.

Developing a Budget and Establishing Procedures for School Spending

The budget you develop for refurbishing will reflect the needs you identify and your overall design plans. In turn, the extent of your renovations depends on the funds you can raise. A school budget of $5,000 will cover the costs of fresh paint, sturdy new carpeting, furniture that suits a wide range of activities, window treatments, and accessories. Additional resources will be necessary for more extensive renovations. Table 9.1 outlines some money-saving tips for library media center refurbishing.

TABLE 9.1

Money-Saving Tips for School Library Media Center Refurbishing

Paint	Seek donations or deep discounts on paint from a neighborhood hardware or home improvement store. Check paint recycling centers for possible trim colors in limited quantities.
Furniture	Look for matching sets of chairs and tables from used office equipment dealers. To benefit from bulk-order prices, piggyback a small order on another from your school or through the district's central purchasing department. Use a bright, store-bought slipcover to brighten up a donated couch or loveseat.
Window treatments	A teacher, school library media specialist, or parent can create magic with a sewing machine and yards of fabric from a discount store or outlet. Custom swags or valances can add a personal and unique topping to blinds and shades. Save a few dollars by removing and recycling old brackets and hardware from existing window coverings.
Accessories	Visit school or public libraries and bookstores for creative ideas. Engage parent volunteers to make storybook-character banners or scrolls depicting various school subjects.
Floor coverings	Shop at carpet warehouses for bound carpet remnants. Educational supply companies offer child-friendly, colorful theme rugs in the design of U.S. maps or the ABCs.

Drawing Up a Timeline and Identifying Tasks to Be Done

Developing an overall timeline for refurbishing will help you focus your work and identify the tasks that need to be done at every stage of the refurbishing process. Expect your refurbishing work to extend over a year's time. A timeline will help you monitor your progress and serve as a prod to keep your work on schedule.

Library Power veterans recommend using the fall and winter months to gather your project teams, begin setting out plans, and raising extra funds needed. These activities set the stage for a refurbishing process that can begin during the last half of the school year and continue over the summer when students and teachers are not in school. Plan to culminate your work with a grand opening in September or at the beginning of a new semester. You will need to accomplish specific tasks in whatever time period you choose. A seven-month schedule would include the following.

SECOND SEMESTER OF THE SCHOOL YEAR

Develop a technology plan for your school. Use your collection development plan to guide the weeding process. Clean storage closets and cupboards to eliminate clutter.

APRIL

Convene a renovation team of eight to ten members, including the school library media specialist, technology coordinator, principal, custodian, teachers, parents, and students. Poll the school community for ideas and suggestions. Develop a strategic plan and consider an overall theme.

MAY

Appoint job captains for various tasks. Assign captains to collect samples and price quotes from various vendors. Recruit additional volunteers. Negotiate tentative work schedules for district tradespeople. Arrange for networking of the school library media center.

JUNE

Submit purchase orders for furniture and equipment. (Do not delay this step—the time period between purchasing and delivery of educational furniture can be several months.) Install the network. Assign four to six workers for a week to ten days to remove the collection from the shelves and box it for temporary storage. Assign two district painters or six volunteers working for one week to paint walls. Assign volunteers for up to two weeks, depending on their numbers, to lightly sand and rough up metal shelves for painting.

JULY

Assign six to eight teachers, parents, and adult volunteers working for two weeks to paint the bookshelves. (This includes drying time and a coat of polyurethane finish for durability.) Apply decorative stenciling or wallpaper borders. Assign six to eight workers to return the collection to completely dry shelves. Install blinds and window treatments.

AUGUST

Assign three or four volunteers to assist your custodian to receive and place new furniture according to the redesigned floor plan. Assemble any tables and other pieces that require minor assembly. Arrange with custodians to clean and wax floors. Place area rugs in proper activity and learning areas. Decorate the center with accessories.

SEPTEMBER

Celebrate your accomplishments with several grand openings for students, teachers, parents, and community partners. Publicize your success with local media, including community newspapers, local television stations, and radio. Recognize all those who have made contributions to your new school library media center.

Renovating the School Library Media Center Space

Once you have cleaned and cleared the space of old books and materials, you are ready to renovate. Just in the weeding process, the school library media specialist leads the school's renovations process. The school library media specialist must ensure that redesign plans will enhance *Information Power: Building Partnerships for Learning*'s vision and the realities of school life. The school library media specialist must also manage the budget to ensure that expenses do not exceed available resources.

Gathering the Renovations Workforce

Successful renovation relies on many people working together to create a new and exciting space for student learning. Although gathering the renovations workforce can seem daunting, many volunteers will come forward if you work carefully with your Information Power team and community partners. Leave no stone unturned when assembling the many hands needed to complete the renovation process. You will need:

> A renovations team of eight to ten members, including the school library media specialist, principal, teachers, parents, community members, and the custodian, to organize tasks and materials.

> Captains appointed to lead in specific tasks related to painting, bookshelves, furniture, and other clearly delineated areas related to refurbishing. The captains are also responsible for recruiting additional volunteers as needed.

> Teams of parents, teachers, community members, and students to help.

Recruiting Volunteers

The tasks involved in transforming school library media centers on a limited budget are tailor-made for community volunteers whose skills match your refurbishing needs. Once you have identified the tasks you need to accomplish and determined when you need to complete each, you can begin assigning volunteers. As you do so:

> Don't be shy about asking people to volunteer their time and services. Many are willing but have never been specifically invited. Make personal telephone calls to make your prospective volunteers feel wanted and needed. Assign groups to specific tasks to create pride and ownership in the library media center. In the process you will build an invaluable network of people who will be invested in your school community.

> Identify eager teachers, interested parents, and enthusiastic students to sand and rough up bookshelves. The more hands you have for this job, the faster it will go. Adults can paint trim and moldings and do minor carpentry. A par-

ent skilled with an electric saw may be happy to create a puppet theater or unusual book drop. The art teacher or another arts-oriented participant may collaborate in the design work and final painting.

> Ask high school or adult education trade classes to complete a hands-on project such as building a story well or reading loft. These classes may also be willing to create graphics for the walls, stenciling, or hanging a colorful wallpaper border around the entire center.

> Use the skills of moonlighting craftspeople for special projects such as refinishing a circulation desk, building a book display cart on wheels, or creating a special piece such as a map or globe stand.

> Check with large corporations, companies, and banks to see if they sponsor employee groups to provide community service days to schools and other nonprofit groups. A group of eight or ten enthusiastic adults can paint a center in a day or two.

> Watch craft store and grocery store bulletin boards for advertisements by artisans and other handy persons who have talent to offer at reasonable fees. Art classes at colleges and special schools may be able to identify someone interested in a special project such as a wall mural. If so, students might work with an artist for a great collaborative learning experience.

> Sometimes, court-directed community service workers can provide labor to fill a mandated number of hours required to work off minor legal or traffic violations. This service is usually available only to nonprofit organizations. You supply all the materials, supplies, and equipment. Crews are supervised by a court foreman.

> Be sure to set aside some funds in your refurbishing budget for lemonade, cold drinks, and light snacks. Your workers will get tired and thirsty on warm summer days. You might want to treat them to pizza or a fast food lunch. They will appreciate your thoughtfulness, and the price is a small one for the support you receive.

Energizing teams of volunteers for refurbishing ultimately pays off in a number of ways. Once the community has seen the results of its volunteer efforts, volunteering may take on a life of its own, fostering further school refurbishing of classrooms and hallways. And the results of refurbishing can open teachers to further benefits of the school library media program. In the words of one Library Power teacher, "The library media center is the place where we all want to be now. It is so bright and well organized that all the teachers see it as a new tool for instruction and for working together with the school library media specialist."

Showing Off Your "New" Library Media Center

Once you have transformed your school library media center into a place that invites the kind of learning *Information Power: Building Partnerships for Learning* envisions, your renovation team and all of your volunteers will be eager to show it off. Plan to get the word out about your accomplishments in a variety of ways. For example:

Contact writers from local and neighborhood newspapers to visit and consider your work for a feature story (either during the refurbishing process or on its completion). Education writers might take an interest in the story, but don't dismiss other feature writers, including those who write about architecture or decorating for the at-home, arts, or living sections of the major dailies.

Plan one or more grand opening celebrations for teachers, students, parents, and community members.

Invite top district administrators to hold a meeting in your school library media center or host a meeting for your own school faculty.

Offer your space for a district press conference or newsworthy announcement that may get media coverage. Any exposure that you can get sends the proud message that your school library media center is special and integral to teaching and learning in your school.

Summing Up

The results of refurbishing are testimony to how people power, when focused on defined and realistic goals, can move schools toward better practice. The changes that begin with school library media center refurbishing can catalyze additional changes that improve school climate and boost academic improvement for all students. Celebrate your "new" school library media center as a starting point for further school-community collaboration that will advance the vision of *Information Power: Building Partnerships for Learning.*

Featured Resources for Further Information

Baule, Steven M. 1999. *Facilities Planning for School Library Media and Technology Centers.* Worthington, Ohio: Linworth Publishing, Inc.

Erickson, Rolf, and Carolyn Markuson. 2001. *Designing a School Library Media Center for the Future.* Chicago: ALA.

Cleveland Education Fund. "A Little Paint Goes a Long Way" (video). Copies of the video are available for $15.95 each from the Cleveland Education Fund, attn.: Shaunna Gunter, 216-566-1136, http://www.cleveland-ed-fund.org

Usalis, Marian. 1998. The power of paint: Refurbishing school libraries on a budget. *School Library Journal* 44 (2), February: 28–33.

Web Resources

Johnson, Doug. January 1, 1998. *Some Design Considerations When Building or Remodeling a Media Center.*
    http://www.doug-johnson.com/dougwri/buildingquestions.html

Libraries/Media Centers. National Clearinghouse for Educational Facilities.
    http://www.edfacilities.org/ir/libraries.cfm

LIBRARY POWER TOOL

Student Survey

Dear Students:

We're getting ready to renovate the media center and we need your ideas! Tell us what you'd like to see! **Be creative! Dream!** Please return this form to the media center.

1. The thing I like best about our school media center is: _____

   _____

   _____

2. The one thing I would change is: _____

   _____

   _____

3. If I could buy things to make our media center special, I would choose:

   _____ More books

   _____ Different kinds of books

   _____ More computer programs

   _____ Comfortable chairs

   _____ Games and puzzles

   _____ Interesting things to see

   _____ My own ideas, such as: _____

   _____

   _____

4. In the media center I would like to see:

   _____ Brighter walls

   _____ Carpet on the floors

   _____ Beanbag chairs

   _____ A rocking chair

   _____ New shelves and furniture

   _____ My own ideas, such as: _____

   _____

   _____

LIBRARY POWER TOOL

Teacher Survey

Dear Teachers,

We're getting ready to renovate the media center and we need your ideas! **Be creative! Dream!** Please return this form to the media center.

1. From a teacher's point of view, I believe that the ideal media center should provide my students with: _____

_____

_____

2. The media center could better meet my needs and those of my students if it had:

_____

_____

_____

3. When I use the media center, I:

_____ Bring the whole class in

_____ Send students in small groups

_____ Send individual students

_____ Other: _____

4. I wish our school library media specialist had more time and opportunities to:

_____

_____

_____

5. I would be willing to spend time collaborating and planning with my school library media specialist if: _____

_____

_____

LIBRARY POWER TOOL

Parent Survey

Dear Parents,

We're getting ready to renovate the media center and we need your ideas. Think about how the media center could be made more attractive and accessible to you and to your children. **Be creative! Dream!** Please return this form to the media center.

1. From a parents point of view, I believe the ideal media center should provide my

   child(ren) with: _____

   _____

   _____

2. The thing I like best about our school media center is: _____

   _____

   _____

3. The one thing I would change is: _____

   _____

   _____

4. In the media center, I would like to see:

   _____ Brighter walls

   _____ Carpet on the floors

   _____ More computers

   _____ New shelves and furniture

   _____ A parent area

   _____ My own ideas, such as: _____

5. I am willing to help with the following: _____

   _____

   _____

10 Community Engagement for Information Power

Paterson Education Fund, Paterson, New Jersey

Engaged partnerships between schools and the broader community are a cornerstone of *Information Power: Building Partnerships for Learning*. These partnerships depend on educators who respect the resources the community offers and seek to harness these resources to advance student learning. The school library media specialist is key to forging the school's connections with all members of this learning community.

> **Guiding Principle:** Different people from the community can contribute to and support the school library media program in different ways, in different roles, at different times, and to different degrees. Become informed about who can offer what kind of help and to reach out to ask for it when you need it. Developing a resource bank of helpers who can promote the goals of *Information Power: Building Partnerships for Learning* can go a long way toward sustaining community engagement over time.

Strategy for Community Engagement

Developing a strategy for community engagement rests on four major components.

A *library advisory committee* that provides ongoing leadership for program planning and development.

A *community engagement plan* that identifies those from within the school and those from community groups outside the school who will help build a supportive base of community support for the school library media program, for student learning, and for continuous school improvement.

A *community planning process* that informs and mobilizes support among many constituencies in the community.

A variety of *approaches that engage diverse community partners* in support of the school library media program and student learning.

The Library Advisory Committee

Community engagement is critical to the successful implementation of *Information Power: Building Partnerships for Learning*. No school reform effort can survive unless the community legitimizes and promotes its goals and practices. The library advisory committee formalizes school-community partnerships. By bringing together school personnel, parents, and representatives from community-based organizations, public and university libraries, businesses, and other interested community members, the committee establishes community ownership for all aspects of *Information Power: Building Partnerships for Learning* and is the hub of all the school library media program's school-community partnerships. See Chapter 2 for details on forming your library advisory committee.

The Community Engagement Plan

A community engagement plan is the second key ingredient in an overall community engagement strategy. The community engagement plan identifies all community constituents who can lend their support to the school library media program. The plan assumes that although not all partners will sit on the library advisory committee, many constituencies in the community can contribute assistance and expertise to the school library media program in other ways. The plan maintains a focus on *Information Power: Building Partnerships for Learning*'s goals and prevents the school library media program from stalling in the face of such hurdles as changing school leadership, restrictive contractual agreements, and bureaucratic politics.

As the library advisory committee develops this plan, you will need to:

- Create an inventory or "asset map."
- Get the timing right.
- Get the relationships right.

Creating an Inventory or "Asset Map" of Potential Partners in Your Community

Community partners who come forward to support the school library media program vary from school to school and district to district. In some communities, public libraries can provide strong support. In others, public libraries suffer from such neglect themselves that they may have little to offer. Some communities can draw on the resources of corporations, professional organizations, and local foundations. Poorer, more isolated school communities rely more on grassroots

---

LIBRARY POWER LESSON

As community populations shift and diversify, make a special effort to connect with newcomer groups and community members who may not participate widely in mainstream organizations, such as parent-teacher organizations or the chamber of commerce. The efforts schools and communities make to incorporate new constituencies in decision-making structures pay off in an enhanced capacity to connect with all students, especially those who may feel invisible in schools that have not integrated students' home experiences, traditions, or language into their school's culture.

LIBRARY POWER LESSON

Allow for plenty of time to develop the community engagement plan. In establishing a strong plan for community engagement, you are laying the groundwork for a network of community allies and advocates who can help launch *Information Power: Building Partnerships for Learning*, then work over time to sustain other reforms your school adopts.

---

volunteerism for ongoing support. As you inventory your assets and needs, look for new opportunities to engage constituencies that are rarely involved in school affairs.

Getting the Timing Right

Timing is critical to successful public engagement. As you design your community engagement plan, you must engage those partners whose skills and expertise meet an immediate need. At the same time, you must also identify those partners whose skills represent expertise you will need at a later time. From the perspective of potential partners, not all may be ready to participate at the outset of the project. For example, a local foundation may love the idea of supporting school library media programs but not have funds to commit to any new project for several years. Similarly, corporate or business partners may need short-term, high-public-recognition events or activities to trigger interest and sustain involvement over time.

And remember, even if some potential partners cannot contribute initially, continue to provide all community constituents with up-to-date information about your work on a regular basis. Then, when the time is right for their participation, newcomers will be informed and ready to engage fully in the necessary work.

Getting the Relationships Right

Relationships are key to successful public engagement. Relationships are both personal and institutional. When they work well, they facilitate the sharing of resources to support specific program initiatives. As you develop school-community relationships, ask yourself the following questions to keep your community engagement work open and dynamic:

- How many relationships can the library advisory committee manage at one time?

- Does the committee have strong relationships with a core group of partners? If the core group is stagnating, does it need to be aggressive about cultivating new partners?

- Who can enlist the support of new partners on behalf of the school library media program?

Once you have considered emerging opportunities, matters of timing, and relationships, you can develop the "asset map" itself. The result will guide you toward maximizing available resources and building additional capacity for your library media program over time. Table 10.1 provides a sample community partnership asset map.

A Broad-Based Planning Process

The third essential component of a successful community engagement strategy involves developing a planning process that will inform the community about the needs of the school library media program and mobilize support both in the community and in the school. Recent, well-researched data—including information on the status of your school library media program and the needs of your students as compared with state and national guidelines for school libraries—will heighten interest and develop support for change. These data are also key to planning your overall school library media program. See Chapter 11 for further information about using data to develop resources to support your school library media program.

Using Data to Inform and Develop Support for Change

A key activity in gaining support for your school library media program is to gather data about the status of your program. Work with your advisory committee to gather data regarding library media center use, compile the results, and present data in a way that communicates the big picture to many constituencies. Relate the data you gather to research on the relationship between school library media programs and student achievement. A community that understands the relationship between school library media programs and student learning is a community that will advocate without much hesitation for better resources.

Using Data for Program Planning

Gathering and packaging data on your school library media program have the immediate payoff in raising awareness of the extent of your school's need for staffing, refurbishing, and developing the library media collection. Once available, this data can also be used for ongoing program planning and assessment. Analysis of the data will take the form of conversation and questions about needs and goals. For example:

> Our school's enrollment is increasing, with each kindergarten class growing every year. But look! Our collection of beginning-to-read books is the lowest in the district. How can we build our resources in this area to keep pace with our enrollment? What's more, the district has begun to assign

TABLE 10.1

Sample Community Partnership Asset Map

Who Could Be Helpful?	What Resources Does Each Bring?	What Barriers Exist to Participation?
Civic Group A	Volunteers; special materials in the language of students' homes	Language; trust
Community Foundation or Local Education Fund	Program funds; links to other resource sources	Funding and time committed elsewhere for two years
Corporation C	Volunteers; materials; money; networks	Contact person may be moved soon

children with multiple physical disabilities to our school. Our teachers have done wonderful work to integrate all of them into our typical classrooms, but the students can't really use the library media center fully. For one thing, they're finding the bookshelves and online catalog are hard to get to. How can we find some help to rethink some of our physical arrangements so that the library media center can work for all our students? And now, here it is October, and although the fourth-grade teachers attended a summer institute and planned an in-depth unit on Colonial America for their students, we really don't have the kinds of resources that will allow them to do much more than use the library's old encyclopedia for research.

From conversations like these, and using baseline data that describe a picture of the current status of the school library media program, the library advisory committee can begin to pinpoint changes that need to be made, identify community sources of support, and prepare a course of action. Then, over time, the committee can repeat the process of collecting and analyzing data to track progress and reassess needs.

Addressing Challenges in the Community-Based Planning Process

Sometimes traditional habits stand in the way of advancing *Information Power: Building Partnerships for Learning*'s goals among community and school partners alike. Be alert to how traditional routines and ways of thinking may challenge you and your partners during the planning stage.

STEREOTYPES OF THE LIBRARY

The most powerful challenge in community engagement in the planning phase is the old image of school library media centers as repositories of books, and of school library media specialists as baby-sitters who "cover" teachers' preparation periods and "book checker-outers." To combat these stereotypes, raise awareness about state-of-the-art professional practice by showing videos about *Information Power: Building Partnerships for Learning* to your library advisory committee, at community meetings, and on local cable television channels. You can use videos filmed in other communities or produce your own. You will also want to arrange for library advisory committee members to visit nearby communities with exemplary school library media programs. Nothing is

more convincing than seeing another community actually implementing the program.

Whether you are showing a video or arranging for a school visit, try to show your partners examples from schools similar to those in your community. Seeing new school library media practices implemented under familiar conditions can help overcome concerns that the underlying conditions for success do not exist in your own community.

SCHOOLS' INSULARITY FROM THE COMMUNITY

A second challenge is the insularity of schools from the community. Many educators have limited experience or training in working with community volunteers or organizations. Yet school-community partnerships depend on everyone listening respectfully to one another and avoiding defensive postures. Plan to work carefully to coach both community members and educators to work with each other. Consult with organizations with established training programs—your local United Way, hospitals, and museums, for example—that may be willing to train key participants, supporting different configurations of partners working together at different stages throughout the project.

Seven Practices for Effective Community Engagement

How do you build on the school-community alliances you develop to mobilize an even wider range of constituencies on behalf of *Information Power: Building Partnerships for Learning*? Seven distinct strategies, each involving a different set of activities, can be used to increase the community's involvement and support of your school's library media program.

STRATEGY 1
Use Community Volunteers

An effective student-centered school library media program draws on volunteer support in a multitude of ways. Begin thinking about how your program will use volunteers by clarifying what you expect volunteers to do. Potential volunteers will want to know where help is needed, when, and for how long. Identify the tasks that need doing by brainstorming two lists with your library advisory committee: (1) the needs related to different aspects of

Information Power: Building Partnerships for Learning and (2) potential sources of volunteers who can meet these needs (see Table 10.2).

Provide meaningful work for volunteers. Think beyond the notion of volunteers doing the drudgery in subordinate jobs. Yes, someone has to shelve the books, but what makes that appealing to your volunteers? Could you tap their skills more effectively by matching them with classes that can benefit from learning from a presentation about traditional customs or a craft-making demonstration? Consider as well how volunteers can contribute to advocacy, planning, and community outreach.

Finding Volunteers

Everyone is a potential volunteer, including paid staff. To maximize your access to volunteers, avoid precon-

TABLE 10.2

Information Power Tasks and Roles for Volunteers

Core Practices	The Need	Who Can Help
Refurbishing	1. Redesigning space	1. Architects, interior designers, university architectural or interior design programs
	2. Painting and sewing	2. Parents and community volunteers, school staff
	3. Building specialty furniture	3. Fire departments, parents
Collection Development	1. Data collection	1. Subject matter specialists for curriculum areas, teachers, public children's librarians
	2. Community resources to support student learning	2. Museum directors, public library directors, university library directors, State Library directors
	3. Technology	3. Business partners
Flexible Access	To extend the library's schedule to encompass more hours and activities, including before and after school	Parents, community, and university volunteer programs; AmeriCorps and VISTA volunteers
Professional Development	1. Grant writing	1. Local education fund, United Way, university programs
	2. Public relations	2. Local newspapers and magazines; marketing firms
	3. Volunteer management	3. United Way volunteer center, hospital volunteer coordinator, museum docent coordinator

ceived notions that might narrow your search. Persist in contacting all groups who share concern about how children fare in your schools. Do not assume that what may appear to you as passivity or lack of interest means that people do not want to become involved in their children's education.

As part of your effort to expand your volunteer base, consult with organizations that rely heavily on volunteers—Habitat for Humanity, literacy volunteer programs, soup kitchens, United Way volunteer centers, and hospital volunteer coordinators, for example. They can help you develop plans for reaching a wide variety of constituencies. Seek help in understanding the cultural and educational experiences of all groups you want to engage. Ask neighborhood newspapers, including those written in students' home languages, to run announcements that describe volunteer opportunities. Reach out to organizations of retired persons, unions, sororities and fraternities, and high school service clubs.

Training Volunteers

Training needs vary by volunteer role. Examine what you want potential volunteers to know and to do. Convene meetings to discuss the ideas with school staff, potential volunteers, and community members. Develop new plans or modify existing plans for volunteer training to match the job descriptions you develop.

Be hospitable to community volunteers. A specific person in the school should be the contact for and training partner of school volunteers. School staff likely to work with the volunteers should also receive training or orientation. Consult with an experienced volunteer coordinator familiar with issues of volunteering in hierarchical institutions—perhaps from a local hospital or United Way—to provide advice on the training and sustaining of volunteers.

> **LIBRARY POWER LESSON**
>
> *Remember that volunteers must feel that their work is important and valued, or they won't continue.* Consider a variety of ways to recognize volunteers on a regular basis, whether they work in the school library media center, as community advocates, or in central planning roles.

> **LIBRARY POWER LESSON**
>
> *Anyone and any organization can be a vital partner for your school library media program.* The more solid your community infrastructure, the more choices you will have. But remember, even the poorest and most isolated communities have people and organizations that can help. They will be more grassroots, but no less powerful.

Create Community Partnerships

Just as an asset mapping process can guide the formulation of your library advisory committee, an inventory of community assets can identify partners to work on specific projects. Hold discussions with potential partners about the connection between the school library media program and student learning using data prepared by the library advisory committee. To lay the groundwork for collaboration on specific projects and activities, visit with them on their site and listen to what they have to say in response to the needs you describe.

Be alert to ways in which you can generate interest for the school library media program among unconventional partners. For example, after Forward in the Fifth, the local education fund in Berea, Kentucky, sponsored a contest requesting help from volunteer fire departments toward school library media center refurbishing, interest from the district's network of fire departments mushroomed. The winning entry itself—a reading nook and book shelf designed in the shape of a fire engine—inspired a host of volunteer departments and community groups to create similar units for other schools. School library media specialists took involvement one step further by recruiting firefighters to read aloud to students, donate books, and provide fire prevention lessons.

Tap Community Resources for Specific Events

Once you have identified community partners, established relationships with them, and prepared them to invest in your school library media program, it is time to create specific projects and activities. Celebrate the opening of new or refurbished school library media centers. Offer contests. Create opportunities to garner financial resources, expertise, and technical assistance. Seize the opportunity to create newsworthy events with an eye toward attracting community support for school libraries. For example:

> More than 50,000 school children in Miami/ Dade County Schools in Florida participate in a four-week contest that encourages research skills through a "treasure hunt" for answers to a series of questions. Exciting prizes and the spirit of competition make Library Power Quest a popular annual event in the community. The local education fund organizes this event with sponsorship from a Miami-based bank and newspaper. Local businesses donate a wide variety of prizes to reward the young scholars. Additional prizes go to schools with high participation.

> New Haven (Connecticut) Public Schools, Library Power, and Fleet Bank annually sponsored a high-profile "Book Bowl" involving a tournament of competing teams. Designed to engage students in more challenging reading, students in grades four through ten read award-winning young adult novels through the year, then prepared to answer questions based on those novels. To ensure broad participation, schools enrolled as many students as possible on five-member teams. Then, during in-school "play-offs," students responded to questions generated by school library media specialists, teachers, and students themselves. Finally, teams from each school met for a grand finale during the first week in June, an event televised by the local cable station.

STRATEGY 4
Raise Awareness of the Value of School Library Media Programs

Raising awareness of the importance of school library media programs profits from a number of approaches ranging from person-to-person visits and conversations among practitioners and community partners to use of the media to educate the public about how school library media programs are vital to the ambitious learning goals many districts are adopting.

School Visits

Arranging for school teams and new community partners to visit successful programs in other districts or observe successful adoptions within the district can result in a dramatic increase in commitment to your school library media program. But, beware! A single visit will not necessarily make converts of those fixed on decades-old visions of school library media programs. Expect educators who are parents to report that the schools their children attend in other districts have maintained fixed schedules. Expect others to raise concerns when you weed old books from existing collections. A repeat visit to a state-of-the-art program may be necessary to convince those partners that holding on to outdated materials is both wrong and unnecessary.

Connect with the Press

Establishing regular contact with the local press generates important opportunities to expand public knowledge about how school library media programs support student learning. Introduce yourself to daily newspaper and television reporters as well as feature writers who cover education in your community. Once you have established a relationship with local education and city desk reporters, inform them of your work on a regular basis.

Ongoing contact with the press will help you take advantage of any opening that demonstrates how the school library media program relates to other education initiatives. In particular, try to position the school library media program's work in ways that will help reporters view and describe abstract, policy-oriented news events through the "Information Power lens." For example, when the New Jersey Department of Education's announcement of new state funding for urban schools coincided with the opening of a new school library media center in Paterson, Paterson Library Power jumped on the

---

LIBRARY POWER LESSON

Consider one or two key community outreach projects that can be repeated each year. Once you establish a pattern, it is easier to carry out the projects and give more thought to the opportunities for outreach they create. "Keep people focused and energized by reminding them of intangible as well as tangible benefits of community engagement," suggests Phyllis Heroy, Baton Rouge's Library Media Coordinator. "We all like to be seen as part of something larger and successful."

---

chance to educate the community about the costs of setting up a new school library media program, and to advocate for using new funds for such programs. As Michael Casey, reporter for the *Bergen Record*, said, "It was just another good news story—'School library opens.' We might not have covered it. But the advocacy around the new funding—a big story we were already covering—gave us a local angle and a *real* story." The district responded by writing new funding into the district budget to support two new school library media programs.

STRATEGY 5
Explicitly Link School Reform and Information Power

You can strengthen support for *Information Power: Building Partnerships for Learning* by linking it to changing circumstances surrounding public education in your community and to school reform initiatives. For example, suppose your school adopts *Success for All* (SFA) as its whole school reform model. *Information Power: Building Partnerships for Learning* supports the model in several key ways.

School library media specialists coteach with classroom teachers, as SFA requires for reading.

School library media specialists can work with teachers to develop lessons in disciplines other than reading based in the SFA model.

School library media specialists will help students find appropriate reading materials as they develop wings and read independently.

School library media specialists can manage the SFA resources through the library, easing the practical administrative burden on the SFA facilitator.

Information Power: Building Partnerships for Learning also reinforces and complements whole school reform efforts and curricula that emphasize literacy for in-depth inquiry and understanding. In Chattanooga, Tennessee, teachers at Paideia schools believe *Information Power: Building Partnerships for Learning*'s emphasis on active learning fits their vision of learning "like a glove." School library resources make Paideia's commitment to hands-on learning a reality for students whose extended projects depend on their access to a wide variety of materials.

Without explicit connections to other reform efforts, *Information Power: Building Partnerships for Learning* can seem like an add-on; full-time school library media specialists can seem like extras; and new practices such as flexible access can seem extraneous to teaching and learning. Demonstrating the interrelationships between *Information Power: Building Partnerships for Learning* and other reforms helps build a constituency not only for *Information Power: Building Partnerships for Learning* but also for a more widely shared agenda that promotes more ambitious teaching and learning in all classrooms and in all schools.

STRATEGY 6
Link School Libraries Electronically to a Wider Network

Linking school library media centers electronically to each other and to other districts is a valuable means for sharing good practices, resources, books, and databases. Linking school library media centers to public libraries and other institutions provides information about *Information Power: Building Partnerships for Learning* to partners working with children in other settings and broadens understanding of the work students can do.

School district websites can advance community understanding of *Information Power: Building Partnerships for Learning* and its impact on student learning. For example, New Haven Public Schools' website (http://www.nhps.net) provides parents and community organizations with information regarding the district's annual Book Bowl. The site also features the results of the district's Library Power Summer Institute, including links to collaboratively developed websites that school-based teacher-school library media specialist teams in every school can use to design curriculum units aligned with district content standards.

STRATEGY 7
Create Community Education Programs and Collections

Special community education projects can also build stronger connections between the community and the school library media program. Some projects may focus on providing resources to community members whose countries of origin do not typically offer access to public libraries. (Remember that free, public libraries, just like universal free public education, is an American invention!)

Other projects reach out to parents to help them use school library media centers, just as their children do, to improve their own educational standing. For example, in East Baton Rouge (Louisiana) Parish Schools, individual school library media programs have set up parent corners with a variety of materials that support parents as the first teachers of their children. In some, computers loaded with GED preparation software are especially popular among parents working to further their educations.

Summing Up

Engaging the community in school reform takes the time, resources, and commitment of many partners and individuals. By weaving together a variety of practices, the implementation of *Information Power: Building Partnerships for Learning* creates new structures, relationships, routines, and approaches to teaching and learning—both in schools and in the community—that together advance the overriding goal of preparing all children to be lifelong learners.

Featured Resources for Further Information

Annenberg Institute for School Reform. 1998. *Reasons for Hope, Voices for Change.* Providence, R.I.: Annenberg Institute for School Reform.

Hartzell, Gary. 1994. *Building Influence for the School Librarian.* Worthington, Ohio: Linworth Publishing.

Krashen, Stephen. 1993. *Power of Reading: Insights for Research.* Englewood, Colo.: Libraries Unlimited.

Lance, Keith Curry, Marcia J. Rodney, and Christine Hamilton-Pennell. 2000. *How School Librarians Help Kids Achieve Standards: The Second Colorado Study.* San Jose, Calif.: Hi Willow Research & Publishing.

Nassau School Library System. 2000. *The School Library . . . Where Learning Meets the Future* (video). Massapequa Park, N.Y.: NSLS.

Web Resources

Hamilton-Pennell, Christine, Keith Curry Lance, Marcia J. Rodney, and Eugene Hainer. Dick and Jane go to the head of the class. *SLJ Online,* April 1, 2000.
http://www.slj.com/articles/articles/20000401_7475.asp

Public Education Network. 2000. *Library Power Resources.*
http://www.PublicEducation.org/resources/library.htm

11 Developing Resources for the Information-Powered School

Nashville Public Education Foundation, Nashville, Tennessee, and New Visions for Public Schools, New York, New York

You have a plan for refurbishing. You have mapped your curriculum and identified the materials teachers need to make the curriculum work. Your teachers are ready and willing to take advantage of serious professional development. You have won the understanding and support of the broader community. How do you go about funding it all?

> Guiding Principle: Although school budgets often include line-item funding for school library media resources, it is rarely enough. School library media programs need a steady infusion of resources. Resourcing your school library media program is an ongoing process and requires a coherent fund-raising and resource development strategy. Working with your library advisory committee and other district, school, and community representatives, you must assess and prioritize your needs, research funding sources, and maintain ongoing contact with funders to win support from local and national groups. Collaborative leadership is critical to identifying sources of support that can be sustained over time.

Developing an Overall Resource Development Strategy

An effective resourcing strategy benefits from knowing exactly what you need at different stages of program development, identifying the sources of support that can help at each stage, staying alert to funding strategies that can sustain support over time, and coordinating your efforts with other schoolwide initiatives.

STEP 1
Identify Existing Programs

Identify programs already providing resources to the school and work with the administration to earmark any resources that can be reallocated to support the school library media program. Do not overlook federal, state, and local funding for technology, books, software, and professional development opportunities, including professional conferences and networking meetings. Ask your principal and district administrators to collaborate in reviewing resources and to help move already existing classroom resources into the school library media center to benefit all the students. For example:

Title 1 Schoolwide Projects, Title 7 (services to students learning English as their second language), and Special Education funds can support school library media staff salaries.

Funds from the Reading Excellence Act, National Science Foundation, 21st Century grants, and middle school reform can enhance school library media resources that support new curriculum units.

School-based management teams and parent organizations may reallocate funds to provide for refurbishing or redesigning school library media space, funding the school library media specialist position, and allocating funds for collection development.

STEP 2
Identify Currently Earmarked Funding and Services

Identify all funding and services currently earmarked for the school library media program. Include local, state, and federal funding; donations; volunteer efforts; and programs furnished by cultural institutions, colleges, universities, technical schools, and community organizations. Explore the possibilities of expanding these resources to support the creation of a new and exciting school library media program.

STEP 3
Identify New Funding Sources

Identify new sources of funding available from local businesses and individuals, foundations and corporations, local professional and civic organizations. Consider, for example:

What do your local businesses (whether the family-owned lumber yard, radio station, or large corporations) have to offer?

What are the stated funding priorities of your local foundations? What national foundations can you tap into for technology or professional development needs?

What resources can local professional, civic, and cultural organizations offer?

Which specific individuals in your community might support the school library media program?

Which local legislators can help identify sources of governmental support?

Search for corporations, businesses, government agencies, and foundations interested in supporting schools, libraries, and/or literacy. Funders often have specific areas of interest and geographical areas they prefer to fund.

The Foundation Center, at http://fdncenter.org, has a wealth of information to help in the search for foundation funding. Information includes founda-

tions' special interests, recent grants, how to approach them, and names of contact people. The center provides free information about how to write grants. The website notes that the "online library answers questions about foundations and nonprofit resources, instructs you in the funding research process, and helps you with effective utilization of our publications and services." You can read the wealth of material at foundation centers in major urban areas (the website will guide you to them), purchase their database of 50,000 grant makers on CD-ROM, or subscribe to their newsletter, "Corporate Giving Watch" at $149 per year. Call 1-800-877-TAFT for information on purchasing any of their products.

Read applications carefully, analyzing the kinds of information required, filing deadlines, and any special requirements such as length of proposals or required forms. Some funders prefer a two- or three-page letter outlining the projected project, description of the organization and a budget. Then, if interested, they may ask for a more detailed plan and budget.

Government grants are very precise about requirements for filing and have program officers who hold bidders' conferences for prospective grantees. Program officers are also available for consultation during the grant-writing period. Funding opportunities for U.S. Department of Education grants are on the department's web page, http://www.ed.gov/. You can download copies of the grant applications from the site and also get important information about filing for the grant. Government grants have a point rating system for each section that will help you determine the importance of each section.

STEP 4
Include Funding Requests in New Proposals

Plan to include requests for school library media program funding in new proposals to public and private funders, even when the overall proposals are not primarily about school library media programs. Consult with district, school, and local education fund grant writers to determine how school library media program needs can be written into grants related to curriculum initiatives, school reform, professional development, or capital improvement campaigns. For example:

Include resources for the school library media center to support the curriculum emphasis of the Federal Magnet Grant, earmarking funding for the school library media specialist as part of the magnet grant team.

Technology Challenge grants can provide funding for library automation, software, hardware, and professional development of teams of school library media specialists and teachers.

U.S. Department of Education 21st Century grants that fund after-school literacy programs can include overtime salaries to keep school library media centers open after school hours.

Bond issues can include updating school library media center infrastructure to accommodate space and technology needs.

STEP 5
Create a Database

Create a database that matches each aspect of your school library media program with potential sources of support according to their stated interests and available resources. The library advisory committee can use this database to devise strategies and track efforts to enlist support.

STEP 6
Plan for Ways to Blend Resources

Based on the information gathered, plan for ways to blend resources from different funding streams to support *Information Power: Building Partnerships for Learning*'s goals and enhance school library media activities overall. Blended funds from different sources can support sufficient staff to work with all students and teachers and manage the many aspects of a successful school library media program, including evaluating and ordering books, keeping technology up-to-date, and seeing that shelves are in order. For example, New York City's Community School District 10 used a combination of local funds and a new U.S. Department of Education 21st Century grant to keep five middle school library media centers open after school and use the extra time available to teach students research skills leading to student-developed multimedia presentations. Blended resources support funding for salaries for after-school teachers and school library media specialists and cover costs of planning time, development of library automation systems in two libraries,

collection development and online databases to support student research, and improved audiovisual equipment for production. This use of grant funds benefits the in-school use of school library media resources as well as extending the program after school.

Reallocating Existing Funds for Full-Time School Library Media Specialist Positions

In every school, a minimum of one full-time, certified/licensed school library media specialist supported by qualified staff is fundamental to the implementation of an effective school library media program. Funding positions may be challenging for schools or districts that do not already have full-time school library media specialists in their schools. However, since school library media specialists serve all students, including those whose needs for targeted services allow for additional support from local, state, and federal funding sources, creative blending of these sources can help support their salaries. For example, Robert Radday, deputy superintendent for New York District 22 (Brooklyn), blends all of the following sources with local tax levy funding to support the district's 12 school library media specialists: U.S. Title 1 Schoolwide Projects, New York State compensatory education services, U.S. Title 7 (services to students learning English as a second language), U.S. Department of Education magnet school grants (building the position into the proposal), special education, and New York State grants allocated for the improvement of instruction and support of reading.

Community-based organizations can play a role in encouraging schools to reallocate existing funds, especially Title 1, to support school library media programs. For example:

When Paterson (New Jersey) Library Power offered to award grants to schools to develop school library media facilities, purchase materials, and plan professional development, the Paterson Public Education Fund required the school district to fund full-time school library media specialist positions as a condition for receiving the grant. Although many schools had no school library media specialist at all, those wanting to participate in Library Power decided to use Title I Schoolwide Project funding to create new positions.

Many New York City elementary schools lacked school library media specialists before participating in Library Power. New Visions for Public Schools, the local education fund that managed the program, found that schools and districts used a variety of strategies to fund the school library media position. Some districts allocated Title 1 monies to the schools or blended tax levy and federal funds for the school library media positions. Many of the 150 Library Power schools qualifying for Title 1 Schoolwide Projects grants used this funding for the school library media specialist position in order to take advantage of the opportunities Library Power offered.

Although budgeting for Title 1 Schoolwide Projects grants is a school responsibility, the blending of a number of different funding streams is largely a planning task, accomplished best at the district or central office where district leaders already oversee budgetary matters. Ultimately, decisions to reallocate resources to support the school library media program may rest with the superintendent. The library advisory committee and other supporters of school library media programs can influence such decisions by providing district leaders with research findings that demonstrate how effective school library media programs can add value to existing programs and improve teaching and learning. Schools not in a position to make their own funding decisions can ask district leaders to convene department directors, including the library media coordinator, to review current use of existing funds and consider ways to reallocate these for school library media positions and activities.

Looking at Information Power through a Resourcing Lens

Once you start thinking programwide about how to fund your school library media program, you will discover a variety of traditional and unexpected sources of support. Table 11.1 identifies some of the sources you can tap. You will surely add others as you go along.

Writing Grant Proposals to Support the School Library Media Program

Raising funds is a core task in executing an overall resourcing strategy for the school library media program. If you are developing resources, you will need to hone your skills in writing proposals, skills that anyone can learn.

As you develop your campaign to raise resources for your school library media program, certain background information will be useful for any kind of appeal you make. Key elements of any fund-raising approach include:

Background demographic and educational information about the students, school, and community.

A description of the status of your school library media program (and other school library programs in the district) and the problem you seek to address.

A statement describing how a quality school library media program is a solution to the problem.

A description of how you will use the money requested to address the need.

A description of programs already in place that support the school library media program and how new resources will complement existing resources.

A statement of changes you expect to observe as a result of the work to be funded.

Keep this information on hand to use in any fund-raising appeal. Then, prepare to make as clear a case as possible for funding, and package your proposal or fund-raising letter in a manner that will bring results.

LIBRARY POWER LESSON

Vested interests and past practice in the use of funding may present a hurdle to reallocating funds for the school library media program. You may need to work closely with your library advisory committee and a dedicated group of school and parent leaders to persuade the school governance committee, school board, or superintendent that blending funds from existing sources to pay for new school library media positions is essential to improving teaching and learning. To bolster your arguments, review research findings from *Lessons from Library Power*, the Library Power Program evaluation report (1999). This report details the many positive contributions the Library Power program has made to students and teachers in schools nationwide.

TABLE 11.1

Estimated Costs and Potential Sources of Support

	Library Construction and Infrastructure $150,000 and up per school depending on extent	Library Refurbishing $3,000 and up per school	Building Community Support Time and Energy	Collection Development $15–$20 per child per year	Technology $5–$10,000 per school. $4,500 each workstation per school	School Library Media Specialist and Technical Support Local salary scales for school personnel	Professional Development 10–38 percent total program costs
Bond Issue	✓				✓		
Local Businesses	✓	✓	✓	✓	✓		
Community Organizations			✓	✓			
Foundations and Corporations	✓			✓	✓		
Gov. Grant Programs (Federal and State)				✓	✓	✓	✓
Parent Associations		✓	✓	✓	✓		
Parent and Community Volunteers	✓	✓	✓	✓			
Reallocation of School/District Funds		✓		✓	✓	✓	
Local Education Funds			✓	✓			✓
School District Building Staff	✓	✓					
Teachers' Unions			✓				✓
Other Existing District Initiatives				✓		✓	✓
Cultural Organizations							✓
Professional Library and Education Organizations							✓
News Organizations			✓				

Making the Best Case

The stronger you make the case for a quality school library media program, the better your chances of winning new and ongoing resources to support the program. When you compare the current state of your district or school library media program with components of the ideal library program you aim to create, you reveal critical gaps in services. These gaps shape the rationale you will use in funding requests, grant applications, and letters to potential donors.

To make the best-case argument, highlight how existing resources fall short of the resources needed for students to learn. First, examine what authoritative sources have to say about the standards and expectations we have for schools and student learning. Then use this authoritative background to describe how quality school library media programs fit in with our larger goals for schools and student learning. What sources can you draw on?

USE NATIONAL STANDARDS

National standards in the content areas establish the importance of developing information literacy skills, including researching problems and synthesizing evidence across different fields of study. Content standards of organizations such as National Association of Teachers of English, the American Association for the Advancement of Science, the National Association of Teachers of Mathematics, and the National Study of School Evaluation among others have published objectives, goals, and desired learning outcomes for students. Reading and discussing appropriate articles in journals such as *English Journal* or *Social Studies Teacher* with teachers and administrators can lead entire faculties to reflect on how the school library media program can help implement standards and teaching strategies that work.

National standards from the professional associations make the case for an effective school library media program by answering the following questions:

What do the national standards and professional associations have to say about the kinds of learning opportunities all students need?

How would additional resources for the school library media program support this kind of learning?

USE STATE STANDARDS AND CURRICULUM FRAMEWORKS

Your own state's curriculum guides and your own district's student learning outcomes can be used to define the school library media center's needs in relation to student learning. State and local curriculum, guidelines, frameworks, and standards for student achievement in subject areas form the basis for the content of student work in the library media center. Helping teachers and students understand the ways in which the library media program can accommodate these standards can also boost their appreciation for the program and its resources.

State standards answer the following questions and make the case for your school library media program:

To what extent do the resources available in your library media center match the content for learning outlined by state and district curriculum guides and frameworks?

How would additional resources create a better match?

USE REGIONAL AND STATE ACCREDITATION GUIDELINES

Many regional educational accreditation agencies and state boards of education establish accreditation guidelines for library media programs. These guidelines can make the case for additional resources for the

LIBRARY POWER LESSON

Foundations and other donors often donate funding to schools through nonprofit organizations—known as 501(c)(3) organizations—incorporated so as to be able to receive tax-exempt gifts. If your library advisory committee is requesting donations from funders who seek tax exemptions, consult your local education fund about how a reputable and established community organization might serve as a conduit for any support you raise for your school library media program. Funders often look for a fiscally responsible organization to assure them that gifts are used as directed and not swallowed up by a large bureaucracy. If you are unsure about how to locate the public education fund in your community, contact Public Education Network, 601 13th Street, NW, Suite 900 North, Washington, DC 20005; 202-628-7460, or check the website at http://www.publiceducation.org.

school library media program by addressing the following questions:

> In what ways does your library media program meet or fall short of professional, state, and regional library accreditation standards?

> How would additional resources help you meet those standards?

USE RECENT RESEARCH

Recent research establishes the relationship between school library programs and student achievement and bolsters your pitch to funders and policy makers that effective library media programs are essential to your community's educational program. Recent research specifically documents the success of the Library Power model.

> Stripling, Barbara. 1997. Library Power: A model for school change. *School Library Media Quarterly* 25(4): 201–2.

> Tastad, Shirley, and Julie Tallman. 1998. Library Power: A vehicle for change. *Knowledge Quest* 26(2): 17–22.

> Zweizig, Douglas L., and Dianne McAfee Hopkins. 1999. *Lessons from Library Power: Enriching Teaching and Learning.* Englewood, Colo.: Libraries Unlimited.

Additional research studies address specifically the connection between student achievement and effective school library media programs. These studies have shown that students who score higher on standardized tests tend to come from schools with more books, periodicals, and other library resources. What's more, students' scholastic achievement is positively related to the funding, the size of the library media's staff center, and the size and variety of its collection. (See, for example, Lance, Keith Curry, Marcia J. Rodney, and Christine Hamilton-Pennell. (2000). *How School Librarians Help Kids Achieve Standards: The Second Colorado Study.* San Jose, Calif.: Hi Willow Research and Publishing.) There is also research documenting the link between student reading habits and effective school library media programs. (See, for example, Krashen, Steven D. (1993). *The Power of Reading: Insights from Research.* Englewood, Colo.: Libraries Unlimited.)

Taken together, research sources that support the case for additional resources for the school library media program address the following questions:

- In what ways can your existing library media program support student achievement?
- How would additional resources help you raise student achievement?

USE YOUR OWN PROGRAM EVIDENCE AND DATA

Your own program evaluation data can also strengthen your case and keep support coming. Monitor your program for evidence of positive changes in student use of the school library media center, student learning, and teaching practices, and use the data you gather in subsequent funding proposals, public presentations, and letters to funders. Nancy Everhart's *Evaluating the School Library Media Center* (1998) offers a variety of evaluation approaches that will help you assess your own program. Her appendix lists evaluation tools found in state school library media documents.

Use focus groups to provide rich evidence of both the benefits and problems of your school library media program in action. Gathering 10 to 15 people—teachers, administrators, students, parents, and community members—together for a conversation about your school library media program can help you track the progress of the program, uncover concerns, and determine needs for the future. Convening focus groups before you begin implementing *Information Power: Building Partnerships for Learning* provides baseline data about attitudes, perceptions, concerns, and needs. Focus groups held with the same participants over time can follow changes and document program implementation.

When convening focus groups, keep these suggestions in mind:

> Select knowledgeable facilitators, drawing from but not limiting yourself to members of your library advisory committee.

> Be clear about what you want the participants to discuss.

> Compose some open-ended questions to start the discussion. You may want each of the participants to write comments about a question before starting the discussion.

> Select one member as note taker.

> Set clear discussion guidelines. Be sure to honor each person's contributions.

> Be sure that each person has an opportunity to speak.

Hold the discussion in a comfortable place.

Provide refreshments.

Following the focus group, analyze the data you collect in terms of categories of responses. Be sure to write thank-you notes to participants and follow up by providing every member with any report you develop based on your findings.

Packaging Your Proposal for Funding

After selecting the organizations, foundations, and people who will receive your proposal, and answering the questions listed above, you will have the information you need to start writing to potential donors. Although your approach may vary from donor to donor depending on the organization's requirements, the rationale you have formulated and supporting data and background should fit any particular proposal requirements.

Sometimes funders require a specific format for a proposal, but when this is not the case, use the following outline.

I. Introduction
In an introduction of no more than one and a half pages (shorter if possible) include:

Statement of intent (can include background information about the need for school library media programs).

What you are proposing to do. Be specific.

The name of the initiative and who it will affect.

A description of the school, or district, and its specific interest or qualifications to carry out the program.

The "ask." State the total amount of funding needed for the program and the amount you are requesting from this funder. Your ask should reiterate what you are proposing to do. Cite the specific interest of the funder here, "In light of [the funder's] commitment to. . . ."

II. The Initiative
Expand on the introduction. Begin with a background section, describing the need and the context of the program. For example, "Our science sections are filled with books that describe how men will one day go to the moon. We would like to give our students books and software filled with accurate information about space exploration and the world today."

Divide this portion of the proposal into sections with headings that explain each component of the initiative: Professional Development, Library Resources, Technology, or Filling the Library Shelves.

Give some thought to these headings so that they grab the attention of the reader. List the components and briefly describe each one.

III. The Components
Provide a precise description of each component, including a section describing the specific activities to be funded. For example: "A. Professional Development: (1) Summer Institute: Forty teachers, ten administrators, and ten library media specialists will spend two weeks. . . . (2) Monthly Study Groups: Five study groups will meet monthly to discuss curriculum projects. . . . (3) Mentoring: Five experienced library media specialists will mentor. . . ."

IV. Goals
List the broad initiative goals, and when appropriate, list the goals of each component. Tie each subgoal into a large goal with objectives that can be accomplished and evaluated. Make sure you say what the participants will do to work toward these goals.

V. Activities
Although you may have described activities to be funded as components of the initiative, use this section to amplify what participants will be expected to do and how students and teachers will benefit. If not covered fully, list past and projected activities, cite relevant accomplishments and challenges, and tie each activity to specific objectives.

VI. Objectives
Objectives state the specifics of what will be accomplished. List program impact objectives in bullets. For example:

Every child will read 25 books per year.

Each teacher will develop two research units with the school library media specialist per year.

The library collection will be up-to-date and responsive to curricular needs.

Twenty-five parents will receive training on how to use the Internet to help their children with homework.

VII. Evaluation

Prepare an evaluation plan that will measure your objectives. For large projects, you may want to hire a consultant or an outside evaluation team to prepare and direct the evaluation. Be sure to include a request for funds to support the evaluation in your proposal.

VIII. Staffing

List the qualifications and describe the responsibilities of the key staff.

IX. Conclusions

Restate the program aims, strategies, and accomplishments. Restate the financial request. Briefly cite the interest of the funder, when appropriate, and how much you appreciate their commitment.

Writing a Letter of Appeal

Sometimes a letter of appeal may be more appropriate than a formal proposal, especially when approaching individual donors or businesses. A letter of appeal differs from a proposal in length, but the basic components remain the same. You must explain to a potential donor why you are asking for support, who will benefit, what the program involves, how much it will cost, and why you are worthy of receiving the funds.

The following excerpts taken from a letter from New York City's New Visions for Public Schools to a local corporation requesting $5,000 to purchase books for elementary school library media programs illustrate these parallels:

The Request: We are writing to request $5,000 to support New Visions for Public Schools' purchase of books for schools libraries. The books, First Chapter and Easy Reader Books, are designed for readers at the most crucial stage in the development of literacy: children in kindergarten, first, and second grades. . . .

The Need: Today's New York City school children, many of whom have no books at home, need greater access to the materials essential to contemporary education. Classroom resources, however, are scarce, access to public libraries is limited, and few of the children in our city have even modesty equipped or staffed elementary school libraries to help them develop a love of reading.

The Status of Libraries and the Fit of the Proposal with Other Initiatives. Fiscal crisis and neglect have left many New York City public schools with inadequate or nonfunctioning libraries. Among its initiatives designed to improve the quality of education in New York City's schools, New Visions has established programming to revive hundreds of school libraries through our Library Power program. . . .

Scant Support for Books Available School Wide (the header elaborates on the need): Quality elementary school libraries are important to sound educational experiences. Up-to-date school libraries integrate reading, inquiry, and communication skills into schools' entire curricula. . . .

Comparative Data Support the Need: New York City spends a small fraction of what other systems spend on books and library materials. On average, New York City's school libraries have only 60 percent of the books and only 40 percent of the periodicals as other state systems.

Practice Data and Anecdotes Give a Human Face to the Data: New Visions for Public Schools library faculty have made their own observations of schools since 1990. Over the years they have observed. . . .

Proposal Specifics: Three paragraphs focus on how children learn to read and how specific types of books will meet the needs of the emerging reader.

Conclusion: Thank you for considering our request. Your support will assist us in furthering our mission. Please do not hesitate to contact us at. . . . We look forward to speaking with you.

Budgeting for Information Power

While an overall funding strategy and proposal writing know-how sets the stage for successful resource development to support your school library media program, you will need an overall budget plan that reflects each aspect of *Information Power: Building Partnerships for Learning* and accounts for the varying needs of students and teachers. Schools with large enrollments of needy students and schools with outdated collections and run-down facilities need more resources of all kinds than those schools with more current collections and newer school buildings. Your budget will reflect both the needs of your program and the priorities you set for developing each component of the program. Remember:

The budget must reflect the program. Funders will check the budget carefully to see if the funding you are asking for is used to promote your objectives and your program plan.

Create a budget that also includes school or district support or contributions in dollar amounts, if that is appropriate, such as salaries for school library media specialists, increased materials budgets. You may also include in-kind support such as supervision and labor costs for renovations.

Identify the contributions—both financial and in-kind—of all supporters of the program.

Developing your overall budget benefits from taking a look at your needs for specific *Information Power: Building Partnerships for Learning* practices one at a time.

Budgeting for Collections Development

With weeding and mapping of the school library media collections completed, the Information Power team can begin drawing up a budget for revitalizing the collection. How much will it cost? Let's assume you have an elementary school with 300 children and a woefully neglected book collection with an average copyright date of 1960. You will need to budget from $15 to $25 per student each year for a three-year period to rejuvenate such a collection. Over three years, then, this school will need an investment of $13,500 to $22,500 to develop a collection that effectively supports student learning.

Depending on the curriculum maps teachers develop and students' preferences for leisure reading, materials budgets may include fiction and picture books, magazines and newspapers, online reference sources, reference books, software, and nonprint materials. Depending on students' needs, budgets may also cover resources for bilingual students and students with special learning needs, including fiction in students' home languages and aids such as desktop or handheld magnifiers for students with visual disabilities. Do not rely on fixed formulas dictating specific percentages of school library media funding to be earmarked for books, magazines, or multimedia material to determine purchases.

Resist the pressure to put "just any" materials that are available on the shelves. When funds are tight, it is tempting to cut costs on books and other materials. But relying on donations of old books or bargain-basement publisher specials will shortchange your program and undermine teachers' and students' commitment to other aspects of *Information Power: Building Partnerships for Learning*. Regardless of the sense of urgency, get quality!

Budgeting for Refurbishing

Plan your budget for refurbishing and remodeling according to the condition of the physical facilities overall, the expected use of school library media space, and the aesthetic standards of your Information Power team. For example:

Given the library's physical condition, is the space merely worn and tired looking or truly dysfunctional for its current purposes?

Given the ways you expect to use your school library media center, how important is: An area of the library media center dedicated to storytelling? An area of the library media center that can accommodate an entire class of students? An area for drop-in leisure readers? An area for parent programs? Multiple Internet connections for simultaneous use?

A budget of approximately $5,000 can go a long way toward refurbishing a school library media cen-

> **LIBRARY POWER LESSON**
>
> *In estimating costs for new materials, expect your budget to vary depending on the current status of the library media collection and the needs of students and teachers. For example, books are more expensive for older students than younger students. The average cost for a hardback book for an elementary school is $16. High school costs are almost double. Nonfiction books tend to be more expensive than fiction. Reference books, including general and specialized encyclopedias, annually updated periodical guides, and biographical dictionaries, are the most expensive books in the school library media center. The average cost of a high school reference book is $120. Paperback books are cheaper than hard cover books, but they will have a shorter shelf life.*

ter that needs a fresher, more inviting appearance. (See Chapter 9 for detailed suggestions on stretching your refurbishing budget.) Representative costs for materials needed to refurbish a 1,500-square-foot elementary school library media center include:

Items	Projected Costs
Commercial-grade carpeting (1,500 sq. ft.)	$1,400
Rug (9x12) for storytelling area	$400
Paint for walls and trim	$300
Circulation desk (building materials only)	$300
Leisure reading seating for six students	$480–$1,200
Rocking chair for storyteller	$150
Paperback display rack	$350–$500
Annual service fees for phone line	$800–$1,000

Costs are higher for those school library media centers needing more than a facelift. For schools that need to create new centers from scratch or alter existing centers dramatically, costs can range from $75,000 to $160,000, especially when installing new wiring, knocking down walls, or adding partitions is necessary. Representative costs for creating a new school library media center are:

Items	Projected Costs
Infrastructure (wiring, cable, ISDN)	$50,000–$100,000
Automation system	$5,000–$10,000
Basic furniture (including computer workstations, a circulation desk and chair, six tables and 40 chairs for students)	$20,000–$50,000

Budgeting for Technology

Studies done by the U.S. Department of Education are emphatic: Adding a computer here and there in a school is *not* the same as a technology plan. If your school library media program needs an infusion of technology resources, be certain to include a technology coordinator or other knowledgeable person in the planning stages to be certain that the infrastructure that links computers together within the school and provides Internet access meets your long-term needs.

The Benton Foundation has a special interest in increasing the use of technology in libraries in the future. Contact the Benton Foundation for a copy of *Local Places, Global Connections: Libraries in the Digital Age* at Benton Foundation, 1634 Eye Street N.W., 12th Floor, Washington, DC 20006; 202-638-5770; http://www.benton.org

Budgeting for Professional Development

Professional development is the key to the long-term transformation of school library media programs. The school budget should include annual expenditures for professional development on the various aspects of *Information Power: Building Partnerships for Learning*. Budgeting for professional development should cover costs for:

Coordinating professional development.

Contracting with consultants or community organizations to insure that teachers and school library media specialists receive the information and training needed to create exemplary school library media programs.

A variety of professional development approaches, including workshops, institutes, monthly meetings, mentoring relationships, and interactive distance learning should be included so that school library media specialists, principals, and teachers can apply best practices to the unique needs in their school.

Representative costs for professional development include:

Presentation Format	Approximate Cost
One-day workshop	$500–$1,000 for facilitators/presenters
Five-day institute	$500 per participant
Training manuals/materials	$50–$100 per participant
On-site mentoring	$200–$300 per day per school

Finding Ongoing Resources for Information Power

Tapping into resources to get a school library media program going is one thing, sustaining it is another. Although school budgets often include some line-item funding for library media resources, it is rarely enough. School library media programs need an ongoing infusion of resources for additional materials. To maintain an inviting appearance, ensure materials are up-to-date and in line with evolving curriculum, and fine-tune technology resources, you need to be alert to sources of in-kind resources and services that can help sustain the school library media program over many years. Where do you start?

Community Organizations

Inadequate school library media programs not only are a school problem, but also are a community problem that calls for community solutions. Civic organizations can be an excellent source for ongoing support for books, technology, and library refurbishment. For example:

The General Federation of Women's Clubs has launched an ambitious three-year program titled "Libraries 2000" to contribute $12.5 million in books and materials to school and public libraries throughout the country. More than 6,500 women's clubs are participating in this nationwide effort to encourage young people to read. To find out more about the program and its local affiliates, contact the General Federation of Women's Clubs, 1734 N Street N.W., Washington, DC 20036-2990; 202-347-3168; http://www.gfwc.org/2000.htm.

First Book is a nonprofit organization working in partnerships with Random House Children's Publishers, Barnes and Noble Publishers, and B. Dalton Booksellers, to provide new books to disadvantaged youngsters through local literacy programs. Donated books are distributed through local programs directly to students. While this program will not build your library media collection, it will get more books into your students' hands! For more information, contact First Book, 1319 F Street N.W., Suite 500, Washington, DC 20004; 202-393-1222; http://www.firstbook.org.

The Junior League has brought both dollars and volunteers to school library media programs in communities throughout the country. Local

---

LIBRARY POWER LESSON

Be alert to all possible uses for the data and information you put together for proposals and letters of appeal, especially in community education and advocacy activities. Advocacy designed to put school libraries on the community's radar screen means bringing the information about school library media programs to the attention of the general public, decision makers, and legislators. Use the data you gather to arm citizens who want to lobby for new resources for school libraries with compelling facts and work with community organizations to make data about school library media programs public.

---

chapters of this organization combine financial donations and volunteer placements for their members in their annually selected charitable activities. Be sure to describe the variety of volunteer help your library program needs from clerical assistance to volunteer "library decorators" to reading tutors. For more information, contact Association of Junior League International, Inc., 660 First Avenue, New York, NY 10016-3241; 212-683-1515; http://www.ajli.org.

Civitans International works to develop good citizenship by providing a volunteer organization of clubs dedicated to serving individual and community needs. They have a special interest in helping people with developmental disabilities. Local clubs decide which projects to support. For more information, contact Civitans International, P.O. Box 130744, Birmingham, AL 35213-0744; 205-591-8910; http://www.civitan.org.

Reading Is Fundamental, a national organization with an active network of local projects, sponsors a variety of reading activities designed to expand children's access to books. Local chapters select their own projects to pursue, which may include book fairs, storytelling and read-alouds, as well as events that sponsor local celebrities to speak to students about ways that reading has helped them. For more information, contact Reading Is Fundamental, Inc., 600 Maryland Avenue, S.W., Suite 600, Washington, DC 20024; 1-877-RIF-READ; http://www.rif.org.

Parent Organizations

Parents understand that better school library media programs benefit all students. Across the country, when Library Power programs approached parent-teacher associations for help, they responded to the program's challenge to improve school library media programs for all children. How can parents in your school and community help support your school library media program?

Ask your PTAs or PTOs to allocate $1,000 to $3,000 from their annual organizational budgets to purchase new school library media materials.

Ask parent groups to develop annual events that combine financial support with volunteerism. Parent groups can host parties for readathon participants; award prizes for student participation in accelerated reading programs; sponsor annual book fairs to benefit the library media program; and develop individualized book donation programs. For example, some parent groups establish new "living traditions" by encouraging students' relatives to purchase birthday books from a preselected list of new books in the school library media center on the occasion of their children's birthdays. For each birthday book purchased, school library media specialists fill out a bookplate that acknowledges the donation, and the birthday child has the honor of being the first student to check the book out.

Promote individual volunteerism of parents and relatives. Many Library Power schools credit their success to a loyal cadre of parent and grandparent volunteers who spend anywhere from one to twenty hours a week helping in the library! Who could resist feeding the frog book drop in a Baton Rouge library? Or entering the castle gates in a Nashville library? Talented parents can make wall murals, curtains, castles, Cajun cabins, reading lofts, and checkout desks, add inviting touches to school library media centers, and create opportunities to recognize the volunteers who sustain the library media program year after year.

Remember, parent volunteers can become your most loyal and impassioned supporters. As advocates from the community, their on-the-spot experience in the school library media center makes them very credible spokespeople for your school library media program.

Local Businesses

The high visibility of library renovation projects captures the imagination of nontraditional school supporters in the community. Even local businesses that have demonstrated little affinity for public schools will become eager to join the effort to transform the physical space of school library media centers and make them a welcoming place to learn. To facilitate business involvement in your school library media program, look for ways to help local businesses link directly to your school so that they can see the results of their donation. Donated paints, carpets, building materials, and fabrics can have a big impact in transforming school library media space.

Do not ignore the contributions smaller businesses can make. Consider asking a local construction company to build a new circulation desk. Approach the local taxidermist to add a unique touch to regional decor. Even a cast iron tub from an antique merchant can become a coveted reading spot in the library media center. Negotiate with local bookstores for volume purchases. Discounts for extensive library book purchases will add thousands of dollars of extra book-buying capacity.

Challenge local corporations to match dollar-for-dollar investments in book collections, and acknowledge any support you generate by pasting bookplates in new materials. The Paterson Education Fund in Paterson, New Jersey, challenged high-profile corporations to match school district allocations for books for high school students. Corporations came through with $50,000 in donations. The money was earmarked to upgrade sections of the library media centers of particular interest to the donors: for instance, a medical corporation donated funds specifically to bolster out-of-date science and math collections for every high school in the district.

Take advantage of adopt-a-school programs in your community or create a program of your own. Partners in Education is a national organization that promotes local business partnerships with schools. Adopt-a-School Partners support efforts to improve learning environments in schools, often providing materials and dollars for refurbishing and rejuvenating school library media centers, including carpeting library media centers, framing posters for the walls, and reupholstering worn-out furniture. To find out more about creating adopt-a-school programs, contact Partners in Education, 901 N. Pitt Street, Suite 320, Alexandria, VA 22314-1536; 703-836-4880; http://www.napehq.org.

Local Foundations

Local community and family foundations are often established specifically to address the needs in their home community. Community-based foundations usually want to have an impact on the entire community, not just individual schools. Many make investments in districtwide staff development, others match dollars for library media collections, and others emphasize student access to technology. Such approaches offer these foundations a way of responding equitably to the needs of the entire geographic area they want to serve. The Council on Foundations has put together a directory of hundreds of community foundations in the United States, as well as some in other countries. If you are unsure about which foundations might take an interest in your district, or how to contact them, a good place to start is the foundation's online directory at http://int1.cof.org/council/map.html.

Other Sources

NATIONAL PROFESSIONAL ASSOCIATIONS

Regional and national professional organizations with an interest in school library media programs and technology are potential funding sources for school library media programs. For example, the American Library Association (ALA) and the American Association of School Librarians (AASL) sponsor national competitions that can provide small grants of $1,000 to $3,000 to jump-start individual school programs. These annual grants help school library media specialists incorporate technology into the curriculum and develop innovative programming. For more information about competitions offered through ALA and AASL, contact the American Library Association, ALA Awards Office, 50 E. Huron Street, Chicago, IL 60611; 800-545-2433; http://www.ala.org/work/awards/index.html. In addition, the American Library Association's Internet home page at http://www.ala.org/advocacy/ provides up-to-date suggestions for advocacy and support.

ALUMNI GIVING CAMPAIGNS

High school alumni associations are a small but steady source of funding for school library media collections. Try sending out annual solicitation letters to alumni groups requesting support for their alma mater.

LOCAL TEACHERS' UNIONS

Contact teachers unions to share costs required for annual professional development activities. Unions are good collaborative partners for introducing the district's newly hired teachers to the fundamental concepts of *Information Power: Building Partnerships for Learning*—flexible scheduling, collaborative planning, and integration of library skills into the curriculum.

INTERLIBRARY RESOURCES

Consider ways to increase access to other library collections in your community, including those of the public library or local universities, as an alternative to increased book purchases within the school system. For example, Project Athena (Accessing Technological Horizons to Educate the Nashville Area) is a consortium of 10 area colleges and universities, the public library, the state archives, and the Nashville public schools, all sharing a virtual link between catalogs. Cooperative lending and free delivery of books among the institutions increase user access dramatically. This is especially useful for technical and scientific materials for high school students.

Sustaining Your Relationship with Your Supporters

After you have received a grant or donation, be sure to *acknowledge the gift and keep in touch* with the funder by telephone and in writing. Donors who feel connected to the school library media program are more likely to continue support over the years. Professional relationships with your funders will also help you keep abreast of changes in funding interests and additional grant opportunities.

- If you are awarded a grant, receive donations or books or materials for refurbishing, or benefit from volunteer services, write a letter of thanks to the donors.
- If you have asked for support but are turned down, consider how a brief meeting or follow-up call with funders might result in your learning something that would strengthen future appeals.
- If you have received a major contribution from a foundation, note all requirements for filing progress reports and file them on time.
- Invite all funders and supporters to important events, including library media center openings.
- Send press clippings or any documents that describe your work to actual and potential funders and supporters.

Invite funders and other supporters to visit to see the program in action. Be sure that anyone hosting such a visit is prepared in advance and that visitors will see an interesting and effective aspect of the program.

Summing Up

Resourcing a school library media program based on *Information Power: Building Partnerships for Learning* is a complex and ongoing process, not a one-time event. A successful, high-quality school library media program must have sufficient staff in place to work directly with students and teachers and to manage the many aspects of the library media program. Just as important, it must have a budget that supports the continuous collection of information in all formats and that provides the instructional infrastructure that will help students learn to use that information in creative, meaningful ways. An effective resourcing strategy is essential to maintaining services.

Featured Resources for Further Information

Everhart, Nancy. 1998. *Evaluating the School Library Media Center.* Englewood, Colo.: Libraries Unlimited.

Lance, Keith Curry, Marcia J. Rodney, and Christine Hamilton-Pennell. 2000. *How School Librarians Help Kids Achieve Standards: The Second Colorado Study.* San Jose, Calif.: Hi Willow Research and Publishing.

National Study of School Evaluation. 1998. *Program Evaluation: Library Media Services.* Schaumburg, Ill.: NSSE.

School Library Media Program Assessment Rubric for the Twenty-first Century. 1999. In AASL, *A Planning Guide for Information Power: Building Partnerships for Learning.* Chicago: AASL.

Stripling, Barbara. 1997. Library Power: A model for school change. *School Library Media Quarterly* 25(4): 201–2.

Tastad, Shirley, and Julie Tallman. 1998. Library Power: A vehicle for change. *Knowledge Quest* 26(2): 17–28.

Zweizig, Douglas L., and Dianne McAfee Hopkins. 1999. *Lessons from Library Power: Enriching Teaching and Learning.* Englewood, Colo.: Libraries Unlimited.

Web Resources

The Foundation Center. 2000.
http://fdncenter.org

The Public Education Network. 2000. *Library Power Resources.*
http://www.PublicEducation.org/resources/library.htm

Schrock, Kathy. Business Sources and Grants. (1995–2000). *Kathy Schrock's Guide for Educators.*
http://school.discovery.com/schrockguide/business/grants.html

U.S. Department of Education. *Funding Sources.*
http://www.ed.gov/funding.html

NATIONAL LIBRARY POWER PROGRAM SITES

ATLANTA, GEORGIA

APPLE Corps, Inc.
100 Edgewood Avenue, NE, Suite 1224
Atlanta, GA 30303
404-522-8640
www.applecorps.org

In collaboration with Atlanta Public School District

BATON ROUGE, LOUISIANA

Volunteers in Public Schools
1584 North 43rd Street
Baton Rouge, LA 70802
225-226-4700
www.ebrpss.k12.la.us/VIPS/

In collaboration with East Baton Rouge Parish School System

BEREA, KENTUCKY

Forward in the Fifth
302-A Richmond Road
Berea, KY 40403
859-986-3696
www.fif.org

In collaboration with Jessamine County School District, Pineville Independent School District, Somerset Independent School District, and Williamsburg Independent School District

CAMBRIDGE, MASSACHUSETTS

Cambridge Partnership for Public Education
M.I.T. Building #E60-156
77 Massachusetts Avenue
Cambridge, MA 02139
617-253-7063

In collaboration with the Cambridge Public Schools

CHATTANOOGA, TENNESSEE

Public Education Foundation
100 East 10th Street, Suite 500
Chattanooga, TN 37402
423-265-9403

In collaboration with Chattanooga Public School System

CLEVELAND, OHIO

Cleveland Education Fund
1422 Euclid Avenue, Suite 1550
Cleveland, OH 44115-2001
216-566-1136
www.cleveland-ed-fund.org

In collaboration with Cleveland Public Schools

DADE COUNTY, FLORIDA

The Education Fund
4299 NW 36th Street, Suite 203
Miami, FL 33166
305-884-2172
www.educationfund.org

In collaboration with Dade County Public Schools

DENVER, COLORADO

Public Education and Business Coalition
1410 Grant Street, Suite A-101
Denver, CO 80203
303-861-8661
www.pebc.org

In collaboration with Cherry Creek Schools, Boulder Valley Schools, Denver Public Schools, and Littleton Public Schools

LINCOLN, NEBRASKA

Lincoln Public Schools Foundation
Box 82889
Lincoln, NE 68510
402-436-1612
www.foundation.lps.org

In collaboration with Lincoln Public Schools

LYNN, MASSACHUSETTS

Lynn Business/Education Foundation, Inc.
56 Central Avenue, Suite 201
Lynn, MA 01901
781-592-5599

In collaboration with Lynn Public Schools

MON VALLEY, PENNSYLVANIA

Mon Valley Education Consortium
336 Shaw Avenue
McKeesport, PA 15132
412-678-9215
www.mvec.org

In collaboration with Bethlehem-Center School District, Brownsville Area School District, Charleroi Area School District, Clairton City School District, Steel Valley School District, Woodland Hills School District, and Yough School District

NASHVILLE, TENNESSEE

Nashville Public Education Foundation
P.O. Box 50640
4400 Harding Rd., Suite 100
Nashville, TN 37205
615-383-6773
www.nashville.net/~mnpef

In collaboration with Metropolitan Nashville Public Schools

NEW HAVEN, CONNECTICUT

New Haven Public Education Fund, Inc.
703 Whitney Avenue
New Haven, CT 06511
203-865-3255

In collaboration with New Haven School District

NEW YORK, NEW YORK

New Visions for Public Schools
96 Morton St., 6th Floor
New York, NY 10014
212-645-5110
www.newvisions.org

In collaboration with New York City Public School System

PATERSON, NEW JERSEY

Paterson Education Fund
22 Mill Street, 3rd Floor
Paterson, NJ 07501
973-881-8914
www.paterson-education.org

In collaboration with Paterson Public Schools

PHILADELPHIA, PENNSYLVANIA

Philadelphia Education Fund
7 Benjamin Franklin Parkway, Suite 700
Philadelphia, PA 19103-1294
215-476-2227
www.philaedfund.org

In collaboration with the School District of Philadelphia

PROVIDENCE, RHODE ISLAND

Public Education Fund
15 Westminster Street, Suite 824
Providence, RI 02903
401-454-1050
www.ri.net/PEF/

In collaboration with Providence Public Schools

TUCSON, ARIZONA

Educational Enrichment Foundation
3809 East Third Street
Tucson, AZ 85716
520-325-8688
www.azstarnet.com/~eef

In collaboration with Tucson Unified School District

WAKE COUNTY, NORTH CAROLINA

Wake Education Partnership
706 Hillsborough St., Suite A
Raleigh, NC 27603
919-821-7609
www.wakeedpartnership.org

In collaboration with Wake County Public Schools

APPENDIX B

CONTRIBUTING AUTHORS

SANDRA HUGHES-HASSELL
(contributing author and principal editor)

ANNE WHEELOCK
(contributing author and editor)

APPLE Corps, Atlanta, Georgia
NANCY HAMILTON

Paterson Education Fund, Paterson, New Jersey
IRENE STERLING

Cleveland Education Fund, Cleveland, Ohio
MARIAN USALIS AND PATRICIA GIBSON

Forward in the Fifth, Berea, Kentucky
JENNY WILDER AND BARBARA GREENLIEF

Public Education and Business Coalition, Denver, Colorado
ELLIN KEENE, CHERYL ZIMMERMAN, DAVID SANGER, ANNE GOUDVIS, AND FRAN JENNER

New Visions for Public Schools, New York, New York
SHEILA SALMON

Nashville Public Education Foundation, Nashville, Tennessee
DEBBY GOULD

INDEX